What Rich
People
Know &
Desperately
Want to
Keep Secret

What Rich People Know & Desperately Want to Keep Secret

BRIAN SHER

PRIMA SOHO
An Imprint of Prima Publishing
3000 Lava Ridge Court • Roseville, California 95661
(800) 632-8676 • www.primalifestyles.com

PRIMA SOHO, PRIMA PUBLISHING, and colophon are trademarks of
Prima Communications Inc., registered with the United States Patent and
Trademark Office.

Library of Congress Cataloging-in-Publication Data on File

ISBN 0-7615-2947-0

00 01 02 03 HH 10 9 8 7 6 5 4 3 2 1
Printed in the United States of America

HOW TO ORDER

Single copies may be ordered from Prima Publishing, 3000 Lava
Ridge Court, Roseville, CA 95661; telephone (800) 632-8676 ext.
4444. Quantity discounts are also available. On your letterhead, include information concerning the intended use of the books and the
number of books you wish to purchase.

Visit us online at www.primalifestyles.com

*To Hilton, a true example of success is
evidenced in what a man leaves in his wake.
Look behind you; you should be proud.*

*To Shirley, a billionaire in your care
and concern for others.*

Contents

PART THREE: YOUR MARKETING

PART FOUR: YOUR PEOPLE

PART FIVE: YOUR SYSTEMS

PART SIX: THINGS TO REMEMBER

Preface

WHY TAKE MY WORD FOR IT?

Over the past ten years I have had the luck to be exposed to almost all the great business writers and self-development specialists. Through my years as managing director of Vision Publishing, a major Australian business publisher, I've discovered timeless ideas that have added enormously to my business and personal life. As part of my work I have studied and read thousands of books on business success, and met many of the writers. I've created international seminars with some of the leading business and management thinkers in the world. And I've had the chance to learn from them firsthand—all the while making notes, collecting ideas, and keeping them in a secret file.

Because of these opportunities I'm now able to bring together in summary the best of these ideas. I've brought them together in a new way—succinct, hard-hitting, to the point—that you can use to make your business, and your life, as successful as you wish.

It's not just reading and meeting great minds that make these principles so real to me. I've been lucky enough to build a successful business from scratch, make it grow, and in the process work with some of Australia's leading business people. Vision Publishing is, as I write, one of the largest publishers of newsletters and summaries in Australia, and one of its largest seminar providers. And while I was at

Vision we worked with multimillion-dollar companies to develop their business and ours.

These great experiences mean I've lived and worked in a world of ideas, and in the practical world of business. I've had the chance to taste both, and to take what I can to make my life and my business a success. This experience has allowed me to move on to new and exciting projects and opportunities. Through this I've discovered that when you know the right things, the boundaries around your life suddenly disappear.

In the following pages, I have brought together ideas and principles that I have found of enormous value in conducting my business and personal life. I hope to bring together for you the best of what I have discovered in my travels.

Brian Sher

Money-Back Guarantee

Thank you for buying *What Rich People Know & Desperately Want to Keep Secret*. The ideas this book contains are powerful and have been proven to work—for the people I learned them from, for me, and for the many others in business to whom I have taught them. I am confident they will work for you, too, but the best results demand your constant attention and effort.

If after solidly practicing the ideas in this book you can demonstrate they did not contribute to improving your financial prospects, I will be happy to personally refund to you the purchase price of the book. For this and any other queries, please contact me at briansher@bigpond.com.au.

As life is about constant learning, I look forward to your comments.

Introduction

Every day thousands of people dream of becoming rich. They imagine what it would be like to have more money than they know what to do with and, for a brief moment, leave their reality by playing "make-believe."

For most, this is as far as they'll ever get with this dream. They'll quickly snap back to their mediocre reality, for fear of stretching their boundaries too far. .

But a relative few—the ones who have not lost their dreams—set off on a different journey, a journey like none they have ever experienced before. A journey so challenging, so demanding, yet so exciting that it brings new life and new meaning.

In the end, unfortunately, many of these dreams are also shattered and all but a handful of people go on. This happens not from a lack of dreaming, nor even from a lack of desire, but from the lack of one simple thing: knowing *what rich people know.*

There are thousands of success stories—many famous, many infamous—stories of people who took an idea or dream and built it into a winning business, and who became rich in the process.

If we can learn anything about success, it's those people we need to look to for answers to our questions. And when you do look at those success stories, when you break them down and find the best ideas and the most successful people, what they did to become rich is usually very simple.

Businesses and people succeed because they do the basics well. In most cases it's not about luck, clever finance, extreme technology, or running ahead of the pack. It's about applying good, proven principles to whatever you do—principles that have been around for many years.

Usually that's all it is. Yet it seems too hard for many people, thousands of whom watch their dreams float away on long hours and lousy returns.

Most individuals go wrong not because they don't know of these principles, but because they refuse to believe they're so simple, or they lack an in-depth understanding of them. Most think there is more to it and constantly seek a complicated formula that takes them away from the real roots of success.

When I present this information, I've heard many people remark, "I've heard all this before; there's nothing new here." And some may agree after reading this book. It's straightforward, with straightforward ideas borrowed from many sources, too many to even recall. To those people I say, "You may be right, but how well are you doing in applying these principles?" Knowing how to swing a golf club is one thing, but doing it correctly every time is another. Just knowing how to swing a golf club does not make you a champion golfer. And when it comes to business, you're aiming at being a champion.

Take time to observe the habits of great athletes. Sure, they may have talent we'll never have, but what they do, and what we can do, is master the basics. They practice them over and over again, for hundreds if not thousands of hours, out of the spotlight, out of the view of a cheering crowd, until one day they are consistently brilliant. They do this until the basics become second nature, and they can rely on them under pressure and adverse conditions. And they return to them whenever they hit trouble.

Over the years I've observed that it's exactly the same in any arena: Learn what the basics are, practice them and use them well, and success will come.

The fact that you're reading this book suggests that perhaps you don't currently have all the answers or know all the basics. You may feel you've tried everything. You've read all the books, listened to the tapes, attended the seminars, and still success—at least the success that you want to achieve—has eluded you.

That doesn't make you a failure, nor does it mean you're stupid or unlucky. It means that you just haven't learned the right things yet—the things that create the foundation of success.

This book brings us back to these basics—things that may have been said before, things the successful already know, and things that almost all the others never do.

If you don't know what they are right now, you need to keep reading. And keep reading until you can honestly say that not only do you know these ideas, but you've made them a part of your daily life.

What Rich
People
Know &
Desperately
Want to
Keep Secret

PART ONE

The Basics of Success

What Are Riches, and What Do Rich People Do?

Before we learn the basics of success, we have to identify what they are. We have to know what success we're aiming for, and where we should be putting our efforts once we understand the basics of success. We have to know what it means to be rich, and where it is that successful people make their money.

Does being rich mean having more money than your friends or family? Does it mean being able to compare yourself to this country's or the world's richest men and women, or does it mean never having to worry about money again? The term *rich* can vary greatly, so what does being rich really mean to you?

Virtually anyone you meet wants to be rich in the monetary sense. Nearly everyone in life wants to make more money. The truth, however, is that being truly rich in life isn't just about having more money. Many people have made the mistake of believing this.

Money should be seen as it is—just a tool for getting things done. The more money you have, the more things you can get done. At this early stage, you must realize money is merely a means to an end, and not an end in itself.

Being truly rich in life means having many, many other things more important than money, such as more fulfilling and rewarding relationships, good friends, a satisfying career, a happy family, and enjoyment of life to the fullest. It's about living a long and healthy life—both physically and spiritually—being honest with yourself and others, and having strong values and beliefs. And it's about maintaining and emitting positive energy and directing it into every decision you make, and every moment you are alive.

The term *rich* can vary greatly, so what does being rich really mean to you?

Many people mistakenly say, "If only I had more money, I'd be happy." Money can certainly make life easier, more comfortable, more secure. It can open more doors, take you places you've never been, and allow you to meet people you'd otherwise never have met. But the bad news is that it cannot buy you happiness. Many unfortunate people have fallen into this trap and don't realize it until it's too late. They reach their goal of having a very big house, but cannot call it a home—it's an empty place with no warmth and no one to share it with. They have a big boat but no real friends to sail it with them. This is the ultimate punishment—a realization too late that they've wasted their lives pursuing the wrong thing.

The pursuit of money without regard to its consequences can be a very disappointing and unrewarding experience. Anyone who is rich financially but poor emotionally and spiritually is simply a bankrupt soul.

Such people are usually surrounded by others who are similarly misguided—who also have few true values. They continue to spend their money in the hope that the next purchase of something they don't need will give them the riches they're seeking.

Being financially rich can fool others into thinking you're happy; however, you cannot run away from yourself and cannot lie to the one person who really knows you. Being rich is about striving for balance in all aspects of your life. Your challenge is to find the balance that is right for you. Then and only then can you declare yourself truly rich.

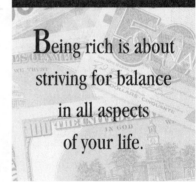

Being rich is about striving for balance in all aspects of your life.

This is not a book for people seeking instant riches. It's for those who are continually seeking a better and more fulfilling existence, who are making an effort to find this balance, and who are willing to work long and hard applying the basics to achieve their goals.

Much about being successful and becoming rich has already been written, but what you may still need to discover is what works for you. And when you discover it, you have to work out how this will contribute to your goal of happiness.

Remember there are many, many blissfully happy people who have far less material wealth than you, no matter how much or little you think you have. Being rich does not mean being happy. Don't ever get the two confused, or you will be neither rich nor happy.

WHERE ARE YOU GOING?

Most people travel through life never stopping to ponder how they got to where they are. The sometimes sudden realization that you are nowhere near where you intended to be can be devastating—and can bring about a lot of unhappiness and discontent.

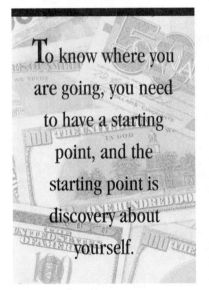

To know where you are going, you need to have a starting point, and the starting point is discovery about yourself.

Have you started to question where you're going? What it's all about? Is success eluding you in your business and life? Have you arrived at the place you set out for, or can you at least glimpse it in the distance? If the answer is no, then perhaps we have more to learn together in this book. Remember, before you build a house you need to have strong foundations or you may risk a collapse. To know where you are going, you need to have a starting point, and the starting point is discovery about yourself. And the question there is: What is it you really want?

Living your life wishing and working for things you think you want because you observe these things making somebody else happy is a recipe for personal disaster and unhappiness.

Your starting point is not to look at what others are doing, but to look inside yourself at what it is you want to do, and where you want to be. This will not be easy, nor may it be an overnight revelation. It is, however, a worthwhile commitment in your pursuit of happiness, and it will only come with being honest and true to yourself.

Listen to your inner voice. At first it may be a little faint. But persist with this practice and always strongly acknowledge your own feelings and emotions. These are your signposts and inner directions to where you are going and to reach where you really want to be.

Do not be influenced by others, no matter who they may be, unless their advice is consistent with your inner voice and feelings. And do not be fooled into buying into somebody else's dream (unless this is your dream too). It is easy to follow others, but this won't give you the sense of personal fulfillment and satisfaction you need to be happy.

Sticking to your dream and being true to your feelings may at times seem like a huge price. You may go backward financially or emotionally—but not being true to yourself has a much higher cost than this short-term investment.

Happiness and personal contentment are your only worthwhile destinations. This, and nowhere else, is where you are going.

SO HOW DO THE RICH MAKE ALL THAT MONEY?

It's a good question. As far as I know, there are only five ways to make money:

$ Steal it or cheat others out of theirs—which is risky and undermines your values

$ Inherit it

$ Put what you have in financial investments, which is perfect so long as you have perfect financial skills—or the right advice—and lots of patience

$ Work for it, which is both honest and noble—but won't make you rich without leverage (which we will discuss later)

$ Go into business—the most effective way if you do your homework and pick the right business

A well-run business can generate staggering profits and will outperform any other means of gaining wealth.

For example, if you invest $40,000 in a bank or in property, you may get between 4 and 20 percent growth on your money each year. If you invested well in the share market you may even see returns of 20 to 30 percent. But investing the same amount in your own business can give you percentage returns in the hundreds or more. There is no comparison. If you want to be rich, your money should be going into your own business.

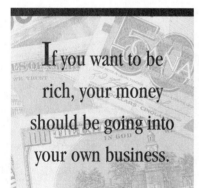

If you want to be rich, your money should be going into your own business.

An investment of $40,000 in your own business could be worth more than $1,000,000 after three years. I see it happen frequently—it is one of the great pleasures of being a business coach. It also happened to me—and it's a lot of fun when it does.

In J. Paul Getty's book, *How to Be Rich,* his first rule is that you *must be in business for yourself.* The simple fact is that you'll never get rich working for someone else. Successful people have always known this basic rule of wealth creation.

WHAT MAKES PEOPLE WANT TO GIVE YOU MONEY?

In order to get money on your way to becoming rich, somebody else must be prepared to give it to you. Unless it is a generous relative or friend, this is not likely to happen so easily.

You first need to understand the real, underlying reason why people will hand it over to you—short of your pointing a gun at them, that is. And here it is:

People (customers) will give you money only as a means of getting whatever it is they want.

So the starting point for you, on your way to being rich, is to understand what it is that people want.

Now this may sound particularly obvious and very simple. Yet not understanding this apparently obvious principle is the prime reason why most people don't make enough money.

People will only pay you or enrich you if you closely meet their needs and desires, or remove their frustrations, fears, or concerns. What successful people do is use all their energy to get to know and understand what needs people have. They do this through their research, their experience, and their own understanding of people. What we can do is to begin with a review of one of the most widely accepted theories of what motivates people.

Hierarchy of Needs

All human beings have basic needs that have to be satisfied—needs such as food, shelter, clothing, relationships, and so on.

Dr. Abraham Maslow was a psychologist who discovered five basic levels of human need. These start at the most basic biological needs and progress to higher-level psychological needs. This progression is shown in the following diagram. Maslow suggests people start at the lowest level of need satisfaction; then, once that need is satisfied, they move on to the next level. The lowest-level need that remains unsatisfied motivates an individual's behavior.

For example, if I am already safe, secure, well-fed, and surrounded by friends, I will be motivated to seek prestige and success. But the moment my security is threatened (in war, for example), prestige will become irrelevant and I will be motivated by security. And the moment there isn't enough food, security won't motivate me any more and I'll focus on the basic biological necessities.

This view is simplified—at any time we are motivated by all five needs to different degrees. But depending on the circumstances, one will be dominant.

MASLOW'S HIERARCHY OF NEEDS

5. Self-actualization	self-fulfillment
4. Ego needs	prestige, success, self-respect
3. Social needs	affection, friendship, belonging
2. Safety and security needs	protection, order, stability
1. Physiological needs	food, water, air, shelter, sex

What does all this mean? The point is that it is people's needs that motivate them to buy, and to give you money. Successful people realize this and always focus on meeting and understanding customer needs.

Because of the nature of their needs, people will pay you if you can do any of the following for them better than anyone else:

$ Make or save them money
$ Save them time
$ Supply them with food, shelter, or clothing
$ Provide them with security, safety, or comfort
$ Offer them leisure or entertainment, affection, friendship, or belonging
$ Give them status, prestige, or self-respect
$ Add value to their lives

There are many businesses out there doing some or all of these things. If you study the most successful people and companies, they have simply done this better than anyone else and made a fortune in the process.

So look around you and ask yourself questions such as: Can I offer a better, fresher, quicker, cheaper, hotter, colder, tastier, safer, warmer, smarter, more durable, more comfortable, more prestigious, more enjoyable, more relaxing, less stressful, healthier, improved, higher-quality, and so forth product or service than anybody else? If the answer is yes to any of these questions, this is how great opportunities are spotted and successful businesses are created.

Find a better way to help satisfy people's needs. This will be the cornerstone of your success.

CHAPTER

Your First Step on the Road to Riches

In everything we do, we have to consider where we're coming from, what business conditions are like now, and what things we have to know before we begin. I found this out the hard way. When you learn my story and the mistakes I made, some key points will become clear. If I'd understood what the business world was like, and applied the basics of business success, my path wouldn't have been so hard.

THE TALE OF A JOURNEY

In April 1992, I opened the doors of Vision Publishing Pty. Limited. I had one employee, $40,000 in capital, and no clients. Almost five years later, the company had more than 100,000 clients in its database and employed close to 100 people. We started with one product—business book summaries—and a brochure. Within a short time, we had hundreds of products and our office bustled with energy and activity.

Back in 1989, and carrying a degree in marketing, I was looking for a job like a million others. Getting one was very difficult. For those of you who have experienced this indignity, you can understand how frustrating and demoralizing it is to have your hopes dashed for the fortieth or fiftieth time. The "Thanks—but no thanks" letters came thick and fast, just slower than the speed at which my confidence and self-esteem disappeared. You know things are bad when your pride won't allow you to borrow money from friends or relatives, so your lunch regularly consists of a shared bowl of rice.

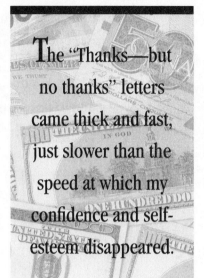

The "Thanks—but no thanks" letters came thick and fast, just slower than the speed at which my confidence and self-esteem disappeared.

Fortunately, desperation is a very powerful motivator. It sparked me into identifying what real market value I had. It suddenly occurred to me that I had been out there telling prospective employers what a great marketer I was, yet I couldn't even sell myself to them. I suddenly realized that the first thing I needed to market was myself.

It was clear Big Business was not willing to give me a go. But Small Business was a possible opportunity—the recession was hurting them too. But I didn't really know where I was headed until I encountered the American marketing author and practitioner Jay Abraham. At the time he was just a by-line on books to me, but since then he has become a colleague and respected friend. Discovering Jay's teachings turned on the light for me and showed me how to make marketing practical. Jay is a wonderful thinker and teacher, whose commonsense techniques now affect the lives of thousands of business owners across the world. So with Jay's books by my side as a guide, I started to market myself.

My first action was to get trade credit—credit from the newspaper—and to put the advertisement on page 15 in the *Australian Financial Review.*

The phone began ringing immediately. From that moment life started getting better. Within weeks, I was working for four or five businesses each month and my income had rapidly increased; so I managed to pay the $879 this advertisement cost me.

My philosophy was to try to get clients quickly to a point where they didn't need me anymore. My goal was to turn their business around quickly and make them money really fast. In fact, I gauged my success by just how quickly I could get them going on their own.

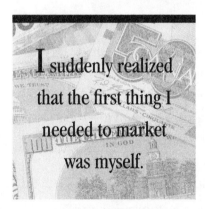

I suddenly realized that the first thing I needed to market was myself.

Out of the blue, I got a call from a much larger client than I was used to working with asking if I would meet with them. On meeting this client, I was truly impressed. After about an hour of sitting and listening, I told them that I didn't think I could help. From a quick look, it seemed they were doing everything right. But they persisted. They explained that, although they were doing some things right, they were also doing some things wrong. They asked me to help find out what those things were.

Because I was unsure that I could help them, I offered to try with no financial risk to them if I failed. I spent the next three weeks observing their sales and distribution systems, and meeting and speaking to their customers and lost prospects. I did discover some key opportunities and gave them a simple report. To their credit they began implementing all of the recommendations with immediate results, which I understand saved their business from insolvency.

At a follow-up meeting a few weeks later, we discussed the value of ideas, and the idea of marketing summaries of business books. This, as it turned out, was a great idea and a good business opportunity. It was simple, yet addressed a basic business paradox: Serious businesspeople need the ideas and stimulation provided by the best business books, but most of them don't have time to find the best ones, let alone read them.

The idea took root, and soon I was introduced to the group's CEO. Together we founded Vision Publishing. At only our second meeting we shook hands on a partnership arrangement to publish business book summaries as a business concern.

Five years later, Vision Publishing was still growing, diversifying, and expanding. We created a vibrant organization that offered busy businesspeople genuine, meaningful ways to grow their businesses, to fast-track their careers, and to invigorate their personal lives.

Many people have asked: What were some of the unique and important things we did to achieve this result? These answers are revealed throughout this book.

CHAPTER 3

Why More Businesses Fail Than Ever Succeed

To understand how to succeed you need to first understand why so many people fail. If the statistics are to be believed, four out of five businesses fail within their first five years. Of those that are left, four out of five will fail within the next four years.

This means that if there are 800,000 new businesses operating today, there will only be about 32,000 left in nine years! A whopping 768,000 will have either closed down, been liquidated, merged, been acquired, changed direction, or become a new business.

The more shocking statistic is that, of the 32,000 remaining businesses, only 5,000 or so—that's 15 percent—will be making a significant profit. The remaining 27,000 will barely be surviving.

Why does this occur?

I've observed and worked with many new business hopefuls, dizzy at the prospect of being their own boss and becoming rich. They go out and hastily start their own business with the dream of making their first million.

If they're honest with you, these people will tell you they started their business to make money and to have a better life. Thousands upon thousands have this same dream. In most cases the dream never eventuates. Most people don't have, and never develop, the most basic business and management skills that will ensure their success.

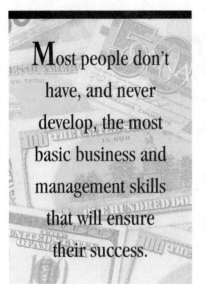

Most people don't have, and never develop, the most basic business and management skills that will ensure their success.

It all begins when they see the lifestyle and the money that other successful people are making, and they mistakenly rationalize that it can't be too hard. In his brilliant book *The E Myth,* Michael Gerber calls this phenomenon the onset of an "entrepreneurial seizure." He points out that most people are trained in a technical skill, and they are usually very good at what they do—technically. They may be a good lawyer, doctor, motor mechanic, jeweler, stockbroker, builder, salesperson, chef, photographer, or advertising copywriter, but that particular skill they possess doesn't at all qualify them to be a successful businessperson. Running a business is a specialized technical skill on its own, which must be learned like any other. It is a skill that very few people learn before going into business.

Most people suffering from this "entrepreneurial seizure" rush out to get into business. They usually begin by borrowing money secured against their entire home equity, or by using their life savings. They invest all their money setting up and getting everything ready—computers, furniture, leases, lawyers, fixtures and fittings, letterheads, and business cards. In all this planning and activity, however, they have forgotten one essential element: customers—how to attract them and how to keep them.

Very, very quickly the honeymoon is over. Most of these raw "entrepreneurs" discover they do not have a business at all; they've simply bought themselves a job, and a very tough one at that. They now work longer and harder and for less money per hour than they were earning in their last job. They have more stress, less time for fun and the family, and are driven by the fear of possibly losing everything. That's the entire reality of their business dream.

The results are often catastrophic. People realize too late that owning one's own business means learning a whole new set of business skills. If they don't act to get those skills soon, the very next step is business failure.

WHAT "BEING IN BUSINESS" REALLY MEANS

It's important to realize that it's not as a great technician, but as a great business entrepreneur that you will create your success or failure. Most people who go into business, no matter how much they've studied or prepared themselves, cannot imagine the problems and challenges they will have to deal with. For most people, being in business will be the biggest challenge they've ever had to face in their lives.

Your success or failure will depend on how well you handle those challenges and how much you learn along the way. All businesses have problems, no matter how good they look from the outside. All businesses need constant attention. All businesses take a tremendous amount of time, energy, and focus.

For most people, being in business will be the biggest challenge they've ever had to face in their lives.

Being in business is not all glitz and glamour. It's a constant battle to overcome problems and obstacles. This is the reality, and don't for one minute let yourself think any different—that's why it's called business and not sport. Taking on the challenges of business as if it were a sport, however, can help alleviate some of the seriousness and negativity that can quickly creep into your day. If you take this attitude, and approach your business with a sense of fun, you'll enjoy your challenges more and find creative solutions a lot faster.

THERE ARE ONLY THREE GUARANTEES IN LIFE: DEATH, TAXES, AND . . .

Change is the only thing in life that you can rely on other than death and taxes.

If you fight against it, change will be your greatest enemy. If you embrace it, it will be your closest friend. Nothing is more apparent than the effect of change on businesses—look around you; you can see the devastation it leaves among those who fail to keep up with it.

Businesses are being battered by change. What we need to remember is that life is changing slowly enough to make change seem as if it doesn't matter, yet it is changing fast enough for you to risk, in a few short years, being left behind if you aren't tuned in to it.

Cast your mind back to 1989—not such a long time ago—and ask yourself how many people did you know back then who regularly used a mobile phone? How many regularly used a fax machine? How many were "on the Net" or even knew what that meant? Bring yourself back to today. Have you tried to buy a vinyl record lately? How about a record player? And how many times do you go into the bank to get cash?

It is said that the amount of information being published and becoming available is doubling every five years. There is more information today in one issue of a newspaper than the average person in the nineteenth century would have been exposed to in a lifetime. Air travel gets quicker and cheaper every year.

Customers today are more educated and have more choices than ever before.

Customers today are more educated and have more choices than ever before. They're more demanding, more knowledgeable, more price-conscious, and far less loyal. Because change affects customers too, they're more uncertain, skeptical, and aware that they're at risk if they make mistakes.

Things change much faster than we imagine. And with that change comes threats, as well as opportunities to build your business. If you aren't keeping up with change, and your business isn't structured to adapt to it, change will destroy it.

HOW TO SUCCEED IN THE NEW MILLENNIUM

Times have changed rapidly, yet we need to learn from the success of others now more than ever. In the sixties, seventies, and eighties, there was a much larger set of advantages that could drive your business to success. Any of the below might have set you apart from your competition:

$ A geographical advantage—if your business or production facility was closer to the market
$ An advantage in levels of technology
$ A legal advantage—if you lived in a country where the laws protected your industry
$ A capital advantage—if you had access to more capital than your competitors
$ A cheap labor advantage—if you could access cheap labor in other countries

In the nineties, and for the foreseeable future, these competitive advantages have all but evaporated. Today we see trends that effectively wipe them out. We are seeing:

$ The removal of worldwide industry protection
$ International deregulation
$ The opening of trade borders
$ A communication explosion and cheap technology

$ Easier access to financing
$ Small companies competing effectively with large companies
$ The privatization of diverse industries

Competition is increasing everywhere and business is tougher today than ever. Customers have multiple choices as to where, when, how, and from whom they will buy.

As a businessperson, you must be responsive to this fact: Your competitors are no longer who you thought they were. Your traditional competitor may have been the retailer up the street or across the mall. Today, thanks to cheap telephones, faxes, the Internet, and FedEx, your competitor could just as easily be in Berlin, Beijing, or Boston.

So what's left?

Four Critical Advantages Your Competitors Can Never Have

If all the traditional competitive advantages have evaporated, what can you possibly do to get and stay ahead?

Today, you need to recognize that in order to compete effectively you have four, and only four, sustainable competitive advantages left, ones that can never be bettered by your competitors—if you protect and nourish them. They are:

1. Your knowledge
2. Your marketing
3. Your people
4. Your systems

These advantages are the essence of this book. It's divided into sections that deal specifically with issues critical to building wealth and success in each of these four areas.

1. Your Knowledge

Your personal knowledge is the bedrock of anything you want to achieve. The knowledge you have and you gain is what distinguishes you from everybody else. You must recognize that the rich, who earn possibly 100 times more than you do, aren't 100 times smarter and don't work 100 times harder. They just know more; they know the rules of business and making money. And they are always willing to learn more.

How powerful is your knowledge? Let's use an example. Say you were driving along at 100 km per hour and you knew something nobody else on the road knew—that there was a speed trap waiting round the next bend. Wouldn't that information be useful (and worth money) to you? What if you knew that there was a broken-down truck blocking the road, one that could cause a fatal crash at that speed? Wouldn't that knowledge be critical to you? What if you knew in advance the winning horse in tomorrow's race? Or what next week's lottery numbers might be?

How much would this knowledge be worth to you? Knowledge is a very powerful thing for those who possess it. Rich people know this and are aware of the continuing need to learn as much as they can to allow them to maximize their opportunities and to minimize their mistakes.

This knowledge, which the rich constantly build on, extends to other areas—such as knowing and acting with the right values. The rich not only gather the facts; they have, and follow, strong personal values that lead to success.

Values such as passion, commitment, focus, persistence, and honesty. These, too, underlie the important difference between the truly successful and all the rest.

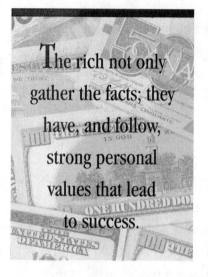

The rich not only gather the facts; they have, and follow, strong personal values that lead to success.

2. Your Marketing

Marketing is your second critical advantage. Marketing is the machine that drives your business. Good products can fail, and some second-rate products will monopolize a market—because of the power of marketing.

Good marketing brings people to your door—people who are happy to part with their money in exchange for your products or services. Marketing is the key function that can quickly make or break any business. And because of this power of marketing, it is too important to overlook or delegate: It's something you must understand for yourself.

The reason great marketing will give you a sustainable competitive advantage is because it's an aspect of your business that your competitors just cannot copy. Not many people realize this.

Unfortunately, much marketing is wasted. You're probably paying the price right now by underutilizing this important part of your business. Badly managed marketing is the single biggest waste of money you will ever experience and one of the single biggest frustrations and causes of failure.

Most of us continue to accept less-than-acceptable rates of return on our marketing dollars. Or we throw up our hands at its ineffectiveness and stop marketing our businesses at all. That is the most fatal of all business mistakes!

Let me give you an example of what I mean. Take two advertisements costing exactly the same amount. They can pull a hugely different number of customers and profits. A simple difference in one ad can make tens of thousands of dollars' difference a day, a week, or a month to your business—depending, of course, on your business. And that's looking at only one part of your marketing strategy. Marketing that is used well is rare, yet powerful!

What impact does this advantage have on your business? Simply put, you can be five, ten, or fifty times more successful than your competitors just through effective marketing. Isn't that where you'd want to be?

3. Your People

Your people are your greatest asset—not your brand, equipment, or products. They are the ones who make your products or services, find your customers, sell to them, and do everything else that makes your business a business.

Yet at about 5 P.M. each night your assets get up and leave and may not even return the next day. When you realize this, you realize business is all about people, nothing else. Look after your people

Marketing is the machine that drives your business.

and the business will look after itself. This sounds quite obvious, I know, but not one in a thousand businesses does this well.

No matter how good your product or service is, your entire business depends on people creating, producing, and delivering it to the customer. In this process many things can, and will, go wrong.

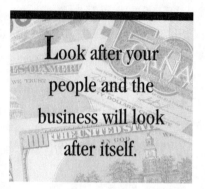

It's only the skill and care that your people take in your business that will give your company the edge.

If your people are sloppy, careless, underskilled, or unmotivated, this will be apparent in the way they deliver your product or service, and in the way they deal with your customers. A state-of-the-art manufacturing facility is pointless if your receptionist doesn't answer the phone properly, or if she upsets your customers. What good will the best-looking storefront be if your sales assistants are ignoring your customers?

If, however, your people are switched on, motivated, and totally focused on serving the customer, you're way ahead. Your competitors can never copy the effect of a staff of people who enjoy their work, who have fun with customers, and who actually care about them. No matter what your competitors do, they can't go out and create this atmosphere just because they've seen that you have it.

Getting and keeping good people is one of the most difficult things in business; it's also one of the most valuable, because it puts you far ahead of your competition and helps you stay there.

Employing people is easy. Employing the right people is another matter altogether. Those people you employ create your business. They create its culture, its service, its quality, its reputation, and, ultimately, its profit. The basic principle is: If you hire someone great, you become great and your life will become easier. If, however, you hire the wrong person, you undermine your lifestyle and the value of your business.

Hire people with better skills and a bigger vision than you have, and you create a great business. But to be able to hire the right people, you have to know how to select them, how to test their qualities, and how to get the most from them. Like marketing, hiring (especially for key positions) is too important to leave to other people.

4. Your Systems

Many people are still confused about systems. What exactly are they, and why are they so important? Part Five of this book will cover systems in more detail; however, for the moment it suffices to say that systems are the only way to guard your valuable time, and to use that time to build the business instead of using it just to keep going.

When you run a business, you need a huge set of skills. Your time is valuable; you're highly productive. What systems do is free you to pass those skills onto others, through procedures and

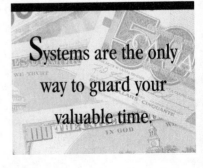

Systems are the only way to guard your valuable time.

processes, so they can do high-value, high-revenue work at a much lower cost. This in turn frees you up to develop your systems further, to make them more profitable, and to bring in new business and more revenue.

Systems move you from being paid for your labor to being paid for your ideas. They allow you to expand comfortably, or to step back from the business and let it run itself. Systems bring you the freedom that probably attracted you to the idea of business in the first place. And with that freedom comes true success.

How Can You Do It?

What is it that this book offers? In the following pages you'll discover how success comes from working on these four areas of your business:

- $ Increase your personal knowledge
- $ Focus on marketing
- $ Choose outstanding people to work with
- $ Design leveragable systems

What this book does is highlight the key things you need to know—things that all rich people either instinctively know or have gone to great trouble to master. It is a handbook for building a business framework that will be worth millions of dollars to you, should you succeed.

Use the book as the resource that it is, dip into each part as you have a problem, and let it remind you of the basics that underlie your business: the basics that will make it a success.

On every successful journey there must at one stage have been the "first step." Reading this book may be that first step for you, or you may already be a battle-hardened owner, manager, or executive, looking to retrace some of your previous steps. Whatever your need, the completion of this book is not the end. It's the start of your journey of discovery—one that will continue for a lifetime.

Either way, I want to congratulate you and wish you every success. For every person still on their own journey of success, many thousands have given up or, even worse, never even begun to try. You've heard the saying "It's not if you win or lose, it's how you play the game that's important." Well, this is true—because it's not how rich you become as a result of your endeavor that's important; it's what you become as a person.

PART TWO

You

CHAPTER 5

The Starting Point for All Riches

One thing I discovered early in my business career was that there is no point in reinventing the wheel. For that reason we must learn all we can from successful people. Reading books by them, learning about their lives, talking to them—these opportunities have provided me with a lot of what I know about success.

Because I've studied successful people so much, I've been lucky enough to discover many of the habits and characteristics they have in common. These habits highlight the fact that success is more than any one thing—more than just making money.

The richest and most successful people I have met (note that I didn't just say the richest) are also the most rounded people, with a range of personal qualities, values, and beliefs that contribute to their success. These people cultivated these qualities at first, then through repetition turned them into winning habits that have stayed with them for life.

GET THE RIGHT HABITS

It's actually very simple to be a winner. Just decide to do it, and then take winning actions today and every day from now on. Real estate wizard John McGrath calls these actions "winning habits." They're what I call your Personal Foundations to Riches.

Bad habits—and unfortunately we all have them—won't just go away; you need to replace them with winning habits. This can be difficult and uncomfortable for the first month or so.

Initially, it may seem harder to develop winning habits than it is to keep the losing ones. And it is. But what a difference these winning habits will make to your life when you do stick to them.

It gets easier as you go along. The more you do things differently, the easier it is to develop new habits. Classic film actor Cary Grant said that he spent so long playing the stylish and classy Cary Grant that he eventually became him. Getting winning habits is the same. The more you do it, the more they become a part of you.

Now you may read the following list of Personal Foundations and say: "OK. I agree with that." To that I have to say: "So what if you agree?" Agreeing is not enough. Ask yourself honestly if you have made an effort to do more and to acquire any of these habits. Because it is acquiring these habits that is important if you want to be rich. If you haven't, ask yourself why. Ask yourself if you really want to achieve the goals you have dreamed for yourself. If you do, and you are sure that you do, decide right now to start living

THE 36 PERSONAL FOUNDATIONS

Learning

1. Practice perfectly to make perfect
2. Have an open mind
3. Be flexible
4. Focus on continuous self-improvement

Direction

5. Dream big dreams
6. Have a clear sense of direction
7. Set goals and write them down

Uniqueness

8. Be unique

Help

9. Associate with the right people
10. Ask for help

Focus

11. Master one thing
12. Do one thing at a time

Optimism and Belief

13. Be an optimist
14. Be a positive thinker
15. Believe in yourself

Personal Values

16. Have strong personal values

17. Dedicate yourself to serving others
18. Be honest with yourself and others
19. Be the first to give

Passion and Commitment

20. Do what you love
21. Develop a workaholic mentality
22. Be persistent
23. Be committed
24. Be patient
25. Pay the price in advance
26. Develop self-discipline

Risk

27. Take risks

Responsibility

28. Accept responsibility

Failure

29. Don't despair at failure
30. Know you're not perfect
31. Accept ups and downs
32. Develop resilience
33. Fall, but don't stay down

Urgency

34. Make decisions fast
35. Develop a reputation for urgency

Employment

36. Be self-employed

If you're passionate and committed to your business, caring about your customers is easy.

a successful life. Commit to making your Personal Foundations the habits you live by. No ifs, no buts, no excuses.

Some people say there are seven habits of success, some say two, some say ten. There may even be a hundred. I don't know for sure, but in my experience I have found that most successful people have thirty-six personal qualities. I call these qualities your Personal Foundations to Riches. I group them, as on the previous page, into thirteen distinct areas.

Why are your Personal Foundations important? The simple answer is that they must be because every truly successful person has most of them, and all success usually stems from them.

If you have just some of these Personal Foundations already, you'll probably have some success in your life. The more of them you have, the more likely you are to succeed on a larger scale. And if you have all of them so ingrained in you that they are part of you, it's a virtual guarantee of great success.

How can I say that?

Let me give you an example. Throughout this book I will mention being passionate and committed to what you do. These are two of the more important Personal Foundations. Now, the sheer fact of being passionate and committed will automatically lead you to do things that will contribute to your success in the long term.

For example: If you're genuinely passionate and committed, then you'll naturally be happy and willing to learn all the other things that are important to your ultimate success. If you're passionate and committed to your business, caring about your customers is easy and you'll implement systems to make your business great.

And the amazing thing is, all the other Personal Foundations I have revealed will also lead you to doing the right things for your success, all the time. Another example: Being honest drives you to providing good service and giving great value. Making the most of failure means that you'll learn from it, and your business will constantly improve. No matter what Foundation you choose, directly or indirectly it will help you do all the things that make you succeed.

Nelson Mandela and the Power of Foundations

Nelson Mandela's incredible personal story shows how Personal Foundations underlie success—no matter how long it takes. The story has been told countless times, and with good reason. It's told because it shows the power of character, perseverance, optimism, and a commitment to values. Arrested as an African National Congress (ANC) activist lawyer in

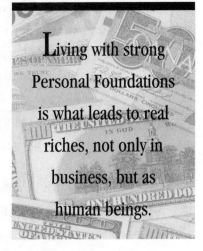

Living with strong Personal Foundations is what leads to real riches, not only in business, but as human beings.

1962, Mandela spent twenty-eight years in prison and stood as the worldwide symbol of apartheid's oppression. Despite his tremendous difficulties, throughout that time he retained his values and his optimistic belief in a final success.

We can see the true power and importance of Personal Foundations in his ultimate success—in a country where he was once regarded as a terrorist by those in power. His Foundations led him to become the president of that country and, incredibly, to embrace his former enemies.

We can't all be Nelson Mandela. But what we can learn from him is the strength an unshakable foundation can give you, and how it can help you overcome adversity and rise to new and incredible heights.

Living by principles is never easy. Until he finally succeeded, Mandela's principles actually made his life very difficult—so difficult in fact, that very few men or women would have the courage to stick with them, faced with the same choices. Mandela had already spent the best part of his life isolated in a remote jail, with very little contact with the outside world. But he kept his dream alive through both his undying belief in what was right and what was wrong and his commitment to the peaceful change of an unjust and brutal system that was killing thousands of his people every year. Living with strong Personal Foundations is what leads to real riches, not only in business, but as human beings.

Making lots of money and becoming rich is simple—but it's not easy. Once you have established the right Personal Foundations, however, it is a whole lot easier.

PERFECT PRACTICE MAKES PERFECT

When it comes to doing anything well, it takes practice: not just any practice, but perfect practice. This is especially true when it comes to your Personal Foundations and forming your habits.

Years ago, there was an experiment to assess how practice improved performance. Basketball players of equal ability were put into two groups. One group practiced on the court as usual. The second group just visualized a practice where every shot and move was perfect, but didn't do anything on court. After a time practicing like this, the two groups came together on a court and tested how good their shooting was. To everyone's surprise, the second group, which hadn't practiced on court at all, performed the best.

This benefit of perfect practice is now recognized in every sport and every field where excellence matters. Tennis players, Formula One drivers, and actors all visualize perfect performance before an event. The difference is amazing. Yet we rarely use the power of perfect practice in business or in our personal lives.

Vince Lombardi, the famous coach of one of the most successful American football teams in history, made a remarkable statement that stunned reporters when he was asked about his game tactics. He said it would not matter if the opposing team had a copy of their playbook (a book of their set moves) before the game, because if his team had rehearsed well and executed perfectly they were unstoppable, no matter what the other team did to defend them.

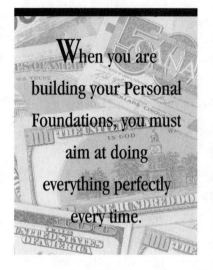

When you are building your Personal Foundations, you must aim at doing everything perfectly every time.

This is a great lesson in life, and this is where the real riches lie—in practice and execution.

When it comes to developing winning habits, perfect practice is essential. That means: When you are building your Personal Foundations, you must aim at doing everything perfectly every time. It means it is more important to get a winning habit absolutely right once, than to do it half-right a hundred times. If you do it half-right, you're practicing getting it half-wrong, too. Look at successful people who get it exactly right, learn what that is, and aim at it. Just going through the motions only teaches you to do something badly. Remember, it's only perfect practice that makes perfect.

There Is Only One Shortcut to Success— Get Educated

At the beginning of this book I made a point that people who earn 100 times your salary aren't 100 times smarter or more productive. I went on to say that the only difference between you and them is that they know something you don't. What I didn't say was that it's your responsibility to learn that "something." You have to find out what successful people know that has made them successful. The only way to do that is to get educated on the topic.

Go into the home of any self-made person, and chances are you'll find a library containing books on business, success, and wealth creation. The question you need to ask yourself is: Which came first? The library or the luxurious house? I'll bet it wasn't the house.

If you study successful people, you'll discover that they all have one secret: learning. A commitment to learning has given them the knowledge and tools to succeed. It will do the same for you.

Cindy, one of my coaching clients, works as a management consultant, making workplace systems more productive. Every year she spends $10,000 on training courses. She spends another $3,000 on business books and newsletters. It costs her a lot of money, time, and energy, but in three years her consulting rate has gone from $300 to $2,000 a day. And she has gone from being a contract consultant to running her own top-drawer consulting agency. That's the power of learning.

When you know the rules of making money, success is a lot easier. And if you keep learning, success builds on success. With this knowledge you can maximize your opportunities and minimize your mistakes. With this knowledge you can *create* opportunities you otherwise may not have seen. With this knowledge you can do things you couldn't do before. It's so simple. When you think about succeeding, do you think of working harder, meeting more people, or having more capital? Or do you think about sitting down and reading a book, or finding out about someone else's business? It seems that the common idea of success doesn't include learning and too often that's where people go wrong.

LEARN NO MATTER WHAT!

In surveys we conducted at Vision, we discovered the sad fact that the average businessperson reads just one business book per year. And that 95 percent of all business books bought are not read past the first chapter. It's not just books that are the problem—fewer than 12 percent of business people attend any training programs in a given year.

So where do people get their sources of inspiration and new ideas? The short answer is that in many cases they don't. They go on doing exactly what they did yesterday, hoping that things will miraculously get better. This behavior explains what makes average businesspeople average.

You don't need to go to seminars and formal courses to learn, although they are great for some types of education. If you're observant, interested, and committed to learning, any event, person, or situation is a potential teacher. Everything you try that fails is a chance to learn and move on to better things. Anyone you meet could be a mentor who can help you.

An employee of mine was working on a very difficult design. On the bus going home, he got into a conversation with a Native American tourist. The tourist showed him some Native American drawings, and in one of those geometric shapes he saw the solution to his design problem. Being interested in people and what they do opens a world of knowledge to you.

Become rich in learning and in experiences, and then all the other riches will follow.

HOW TO STAY POOR—GUARANTEED

The two biggest enemies of learning are comfort and arrogance—either will cripple your desire to learn and grow. And when you don't learn and grow, success will not only be hard to come by, it will positively avoid you.

Become rich in learning and in experiences, and then all the other riches will follow.

The fact that you are reading this book means you have already understood at least part of this message. But in business today, I can assure you that this problem is chronic. That's true not only for people who need to educate themselves, but also for those responsible for educating their staff.

I have worked with business owners who've complained that their salespeople weren't doing the job, but who didn't give those salespeople any training or support to develop their skills. The owners didn't even bother to ensure that their own sales and marketing skills were up to snuff. They felt they knew enough. Through their arrogance they closed off their own development and that of their staff. The only way for their business to go was down.

COMFORT: THE NATURAL ENEMY OF THE RICH

There are those in business who feel that even if they don't know it all, they're doing all right. They don't, or won't, make the effort to learn because they're too comfortable. Without the pressure of losses, or obvious failures, they won't do anything different. This is a certain path to lifelong mediocrity.

In the last fifteen years, many businesspeople have come across the idea of continuous improvement. The basic idea is to always work to do things better. This still makes sense. And it's equally important for individuals. You want to succeed as a business? You have to work outside your comfort zone to keep getting better. You want to succeed as an individual? You have to work outside your comfort zone to keep getting better.

Put time aside to learn something new and put your Personal Foundations into action every day. Not only will you be a more fulfilled person, but you'll be miles in front of your competitors who just stay comfortable and do the same thing all the time.

Put time aside to learn something new and put your Personal Foundations into action every day.

Read business books, read summaries, read business magazines, listen to tapes of successful people, watch business videos, attend seminars, go out and see what your competitors are doing. Get involved. Get educated—every day.

IT'S NOT WHERE YOU START, IT'S WHERE YOU FINISH THAT COUNTS

In our lives, some of us get dealt a great hand of cards at the start, others a bad one. But as in any game, it's not always the best hand that wins, it's the best player who does.

Personal improvement is about becoming the best player possible. It's about growing, it's about fulfillment, it's about self-respect and confidence. This means different things to different people. It doesn't matter. For some people conquering the highest mountain is not enough, but for others just being able to get out of bed in the morning and walk to the garden is a huge achievement.

What's important is that you always strive to give your best, and be the best person you can be, regardless of what your hand is at the start. Because when you adopt this attitude, you'll find that the hand you're dealt becomes less important, compared with the hand that will end up winning the game.

Personal development is your only guaranteed path to success, and each step you take along that path is something that can never be taken away from you.

TAKE THE TIME TO TEACH, AND YOU'LL LEARN MORE THAN YOU CAN IMAGINE

When we teach, we also learn. The old saying "Those who can, do; those who can't, teach" is wide of the mark. Look around in your own life and you'll see that the best teachers are often the best at what they do. A classic example is the genius physicist Albert Einstein: not only a great teacher in his own field, but a great communicator of his ideas to ordinary people. Part of being great at what you do is also being able to help others do it too. When you teach, you automatically expand your vision, and that helps you see things differently. And every time we see differently, we learn something.

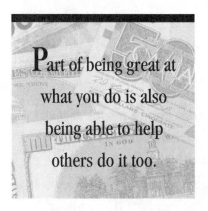

Part of being great at what you do is also being able to help others do it too.

In business, successful people impart knowledge to those they work with. They understand that doing that builds their business, builds their people, and exposes them to new ways of doing things.

If you've ever spent time with a questioning child, you'll know what I mean. If you even go close to answering all their questions, you'll have learned a whole lot more.

WHY MOST PEOPLE END UP WITH NO MONEY

Statisticians tell us that only around 5 percent of people will retire independently wealthy. This means that only 5 percent of sixty-five-year-olds can support themselves without government or family assistance. This is a really dismal and depressing statistic—especially as you start to creep past forty or fifty.

No one seems to have asked the important question: "Why?" What is it that makes financial independence so difficult to attain?

The simple answer is that most people have never been taught how to:

$ Earn enough money
$ Keep it
$ Use it effectively during their lifetime

IF YOU WANT TO BE RICH AND HAPPY, DON'T GO TO SCHOOL

In developed countries we all receive a basic education that teaches us to read, write, and do mathematics. Then we're thrown out into the world, either to sit in a salaried job, to join the ever-growing ranks of the unemployed, or to start businesses that are likely to fail. We are basically cut loose without any skills in securing a job, and with no idea of how to be in business for ourselves.

If this says anything, it says our formal education system has let us down. It doesn't give us important life skills. School for me meant following the traditional rules, giving people only what they expected, and getting ahead by doing the same things as everyone else. I wouldn't call that a recipe for success.

At no stage are we taught how to get a job, or how to earn, keep, and use money correctly. Rarely are these things talked about at our schools and universities. Even some of the most highly regarded business courses skirt around the issue. They teach students "soft" skills, hoping that when they get out into the real world they'll be able to figure it out for themselves.

THE TRUTH ABOUT EDUCATION AND SUCCESS

Studies of individuals who have above-average wealth show no real correlation between levels of formal education and the ability to make money. Formal education may affect how much you make in a salaried job, but it doesn't affect your chances of real financial independence.

If you look a little closer, however, there is a very strong correlation between one type of education and wealth. Those who have acquired wealth are all well educated in the art of making money. This "education" wasn't acquired at a conventional school or university. These people gained it at the "School of Wealth."

Attend Only the School of Wealth

Jason was an average student at school, who acquired a certificate in training and got a job as a trainer in a major firm.
After about five years he was earning roughly $40,000 a
year and was doing OK. After about eight years he was
earning $50,000 a year and was paying off a house. Then he
started his own training business and retired in three years—
at age thirty.

Jason was pretty mediocre in all the usual measures of
school success. No one would have picked him as someone
who would retire at thirty, but he had something that made
the difference. He knew, and did,
many of the right things for developing wealth.

Wealth education is difficult
to get. The problem is that no formal school of wealth exists.
Wealth education is usually acquired by trial and error, by risk-
taking, by losses and wins. This
can be very time consuming and
very costly, both financially and

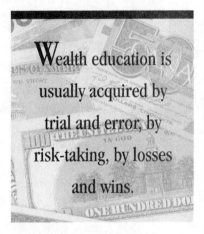

Wealth education is usually acquired by trial and error, by risk-taking, by losses and wins.

emotionally. Every owner of a failed business can vouch for
that. The only way to avoid these costly mistakes is to find a
successful person who will pass this education on to you.

However, having it passed on to you is very rare. The
people who have this knowledge are too few, and too busy,
to be able to stop and help others learn. The people who
desperately need wealth education cannot afford to pay the
right teachers what they are worth. And unfortunately, these

skills can't be picked up overnight. They usually require intimate knowledge and can take years to learn.

To make it worse, in our world of instant gratification, most people don't see an investment in their education as something worthwhile, especially when the payoff could take more than ten years. It all becomes too hard. It is much easier to sell your time in short bursts of a week or so and collect a paycheck.

If You Want to Be Rich, Study Success and Nothing Else

Jason started his working life by falling into the trap of only seeing the short term, but he soon learned that investing in his education was priceless. He made it his business to learn from people who were already doing well. This behavior is called "modeling." You identify people who do things well, figure out how they do it, and then copy them. It sounds simple, but it takes time. Jason picked out people whose

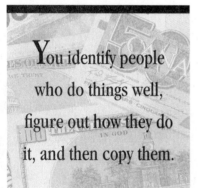

You identify people who do things well, figure out how they do it, and then copy them.

lives and businesses he admired, figured out the strategies they used, and applied them to his life. You've seen the results from salary slave to financial independence in three years.

The easiest thing you can do is read a successful person's autobiography. But if you are more resourceful, you'll get to meet and learn from these people directly. It's a secret that's been around since civilization began. From Chinese martial arts to Renaissance painting, students have always learned by emulating the masters.

This is your only shortcut to success. Model the successes of people you admire and learn from their mistakes. These people are the ones who have done it all and can give you invaluable advice on how to earn, keep, and use money. It's a price worth paying, no matter how outlandish the cost may seem at the time.

CHAPTER 7

Dream
Big Dreams

A friend of mine has more talent than I can imagine having. Over the years, I've watched him pick up things
easily, change careers comfortably, and develop skills without seeming to try. But it is only now, at thirty-two, that he
is taking his first steps toward success. Up to now he has
simply bumbled along because he never had anything he really wanted.

With a dream, however, success comes much more easily.
Dream a dream that excites you. Focus on it exclusively.
Hang onto it regardless of the people who try to tear it
down.

If you don't have a dream of your own, you'll work all
your life to fulfill someone else's dream. Dreaming costs you
nothing, while not dreaming will cost you everything. Without a dream you cannot have a goal. Without a goal you'll
never take any positive action. Without any positive action,
nothing will happen to bring you any closer to your dream.

If you're going to dream, you may as well dream big.
The bigger your dream, the more excited and motivated you

will be to actually begin on the road to reaching it. An exciting dream motivates us and keeps us going when things get difficult. If you always have that dream in mind, everything you do will take you closer to your goal. James Collins and Jerry Pores, in their

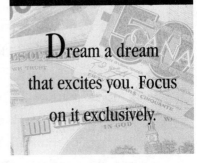

Dream a dream that excites you. Focus on it exclusively.

book *Built to Last,* describe corporate success as stemming from "Big Hairy Audacious Goals." It's the same for individuals—if you dream big, you win big.

Whatever you think of the Amway system, they've got one thing exactly right: Every person who comes into their organization is encouraged to dream. In fact, they are almost taught to dream, to set their direction, to build on goals that take them where they want to go. The company supports all this through systems of recognition that make successful dreaming a model for everyone. You can easily see the effect in their commitment, creativity, and passion for their work. Some people may not like the way they recruit, but the way they nurture their dreams and passion is an example we all could follow.

BEWARE OF THE DREAMTAKERS

As young children we naturally have wild and wonderful imaginations and can easily picture how our lives could be. We all have the capacity to "make believe" and build a dream world for ourselves. But as we grow older, we unfortunately and inevitably run into some very dangerous people. These aren't violent criminals, but nice people who can cause us immense damage.

Tom O'Toole runs the phenomenally successful Beechworth Bakery in Victoria. The town of Beechworth has a population of only 3,700, but this business attracts customers statewide, making it the busiest bakery with the highest turnover in all Victoria. Tom has no business or management training yet is invited to speak to businesspeople from all over the country. He uses the term "Dream-Takers" to describe those people who have lost their own dreams long ago, and who through their negativity destroy the dreams of those around them.

Beware: DreamTakers are everywhere. They are the people who constantly tell us we cannot do things, that we should be careful "not to fail." These people may be our friends, relatives, parents, or teachers. They may be total strangers. We have to be vigilant and ensure they don't influence our thinking in any way.

A participant at one of my seminars told a story of a DreamTaker. As a teenager he was interested in music and often played around with his singing. One day he was singing to himself when his mother started to laugh at him. In retrospect, he could smile and say that his voice was breaking, and that it probably sounded pretty funny. But even as he told the story, a blush came to his face. All those years ago, he had shown his dream without protecting it, and

Try to find dream builders—positive, successful people— to be with.

someone had trampled on it. He finished the story by saying he'd never thought about singing again.

This sort of scenario is pretty typical. However, if it does happen, it doesn't mean you should hide yourself away or that you shouldn't share your dreams. Sharing your dreams is an important part of making them real. It simply means that you have to take care of them and avoid the DreamTakers. Remember that things always rub off the people you're with. Try to find dream builders—positive, successful people—to be with. And where you can't avoid DreamTakers, build barriers to keep your dream safe.

DECIDE WHERE YOU'RE HEADED

Direction is central to becoming rich. When you have your dream, you can then decide in what direction you're headed.

Translate your dream into some easily definable short-term goal in a series of easy-to-accomplish steps that you can visualize. Put these goals in writing. Put them in a place where you can refer to them every day. Do not be afraid to share these with people you trust to be supportive, to help guide you. Start talking to people about how to reach your goals. All these things make your dream and your goals more real. They make your commitment real, rather than just being something buried in your head that you can easily forget.

This is where most people go wrong. They don't know what they want. Without making that choice, people end up with whatever life gives them. And that gift is rarely riches.

Set clear, realistic goals Goals provide focus and direction, and with them many things that seem difficult become

It's always better to set a single life goal and achieve it.

easy. With clear goals, the steps to your dream often seem to just fall into place. Without goals, it can be impossible to decide what you need to do.

Someone once said that people spend more time thinking about their shopping list than they do about their life goals. If it's true, it's very sad. It's always better to set a single life goal and achieve it. Compare that with setting no goal, or a hundred goals, and achieving nothing with your life.

My talented friend has only just learned this. He sort of understood, spending his life committing to mini-goals that he worked at and achieved. He was a scratch golfer. He could speak French. He could do a hundred other things, but they were things that just popped up in his field of vision that he thought he'd try. It wasn't until his thirties that he actually chose to work at something because it was what he wanted to do with his life.

RICH PEOPLE ARE ALWAYS WILLING TO PAY THE PRICE

When you have your goal, figure out what price you'll have to pay to achieve it. Everything worthwhile has some sort of price. It may be you need to give up your time, your sporting career, your illusions of perfection, or a big salary in another career.

Decide now what you are willing to give up to achieve your goal, then pay that price and pay it without hesitation or regret.

Be Unique or
Be Nothing at All

Mediocre, part of the crowd, anonymous, average. This is the result of not being unique or, even worse, not recognizing your uniqueness.

We are all unique in some special way, but most of us have been taught, pushed, and punished into conformity. We are told not to stick our necks out too far and not to make too much noise in case we are noticed.

In Australia we have the tall-poppy syndrome, always looming for those who dare to succeed. Our culture is such that people will try to chop your head off if you grow too big. Yet ironically, society rewards uniqueness in skills and talents in business, sport, art, and culture. These two things, the rewards on the one hand and the tall-poppy syndrome on the other, don't seem to belong together. But it makes sense when you realize that being unique means making the conscious and definite choice to go against the grain and risk sticking your neck out. People who succeed have to be resilient and courageous to go against the grain, to be nonconformist, and to be unique in the face of peer pressure. In our society there are many barriers to putting yourself forward and being unique. This is one reason why society respects qualities such as uniqueness, outstanding talent, and courage.

When I suggest to my clients that they must "be unique," they often look at me blankly. Too often businesspeople are ready to accept that they, and their business, are nothing special—not unique in any way, just another "me too" business—that they have nothing unique to offer. But by accepting this, they have condemned themselves to being mediocre. Your uniqueness is what makes you stand out. It's what makes people choose you rather than another person to deal with, or select your business rather than a competitor's.

What is unique about you or about your business? What is it that makes your business different? Find it, develop it, and use it every day. Successful people know the power of uniqueness and make sure they use it. This idea of uniqueness is so important that I will look at it again in great detail when I discuss marketing in Part Five.

CHAPTER

Ask for Help—
You'll Be Surprised
at What Will Happen

You'll be surprised who will help you, if you simply ask. Brett Kelly, a young Australian author, tells a great story of putting together his first book. A struggling writer with no job, no money, no publisher, and no contacts, he phoned a publishing expert to get some advice. Days later he had an editor, a book designer, a publicist, and a distributor, most of whom were willing to work for nothing. But he still had to pay for the printing. After a few phone calls, he had ten patrons each putting up money to publish it. And all he had done was ask for some help.

When you're genuine about what you are asking for, and if you ask in the right way, you'll be amazed at who'll be prepared to help. Although you can't expect people to help you for nothing, many of them will. But for those who do charge, you should always be happy to pay for the help—it's only fair.

You should also recognize that you don't have to reach success on your own. In fact, you can't do it on your own. Having the courage to ask for help is a characteristic of all successful people. It isn't a sign of weakness, but a sign of strength. Success is something people build together, and asking for help is a solid step toward it.

IF YOU WANT FLEAS, LIE WITH DOGS

Success is a joint effort; few people are truly self-made. Every successful person has had help, has had a mentor or coach, or has had a team supporting him. But that support doesn't come from just anyone. Successful people surround themselves with successes, just as losers tend to hang together too.

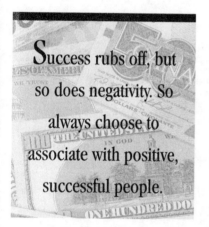

Success rubs off, but so does negativity. So always choose to associate with positive, successful people.

That doesn't mean all your friends have to be rich. Success is about more than money. It's about attitude; it's about reaching for your dreams; it's about building people up, not tearing them down. Success rubs off, but so does negativity. So always choose to associate with positive, successful people.

This is what can be said of my meeting with marketing guru Jay Abraham. After working with Jay, and later becoming a friend, I learned more about marketing than I thought possible. I learned what works and what doesn't, and why. This was possible only because I had the opportunity to be around supportive people like Jay to act as mentors in my own life.

Do You Want to Be a Business Champion? Then Get a Business Coach!

Why do top athletes like Pete Sampras, Michael Jordan, Evander Holyfield, and Kieren Perkins travel the world with their coaches? Why do the best in the world need a coach at all? Because coaches play a vital role in their successes. Playing at peak performance day in and day out is difficult and draining. Coaches advise, cajole, demonstrate, and inspire them to perform better. Coaches give players new and different perspectives on what they do and help them to continually improve. Despite this lesson, most people in business, especially small business, feel they must make their journey alone.

Being in business can be a lonely place. Big companies have boards of directors, consultants, and advisers. There are hordes of people to provide specialized advice, perspective, and objectivity.

When you're in your own business, you're out there alone. Without a coach or mentor, you can struggle unnecessarily with decisions and problems someone else has experienced and solved.

Don't waste your time reinventing the wheel. You're better off using your time to generate sales and revenue. When you struggle with a problem someone else can solve faster, you're costing your business a lot of money.

Hiring someone as your business coach will also cost you money—but it's money well spent. A good business coach can make you a fortune by helping you avoid costly mistakes and by maximizing opportunities. A coach's fee is an investment. Like every other investment, the risks vary according to the quality of the product. You wouldn't buy a poor property with low return simply because it's cheap. So don't make that mistake with a coach—get the best coach you can afford, one who knows your business and area. Listen carefully. You'll get your money back, and more.

Having a business coach or mentor isn't optional anymore. It's essential if you want to succeed and create the business you have always hoped for. No one can take up a new sport and expect to win without lessons from someone who knows what they're doing. Building a business is no different.

Is Your Name Poor Jack or Rich Michael?

Most people are jacks-of-all-trades and masters of none. They're happy doing lots of different things badly; because they're easily bored, they can't choose or they don't understand how important focus is. Focus is essential. You are always better off being an expert in one thing rather than average at everything.

People confuse this focus with limiting themselves. In the short term, being focused means you don't do other things—that you concentrate on the one thing you're really good at. So I suppose it is a kind of limitation. But the success that comes with that focus will open many more doors for you. In fact, it opens more doors than you could have imagined before succeeding.

We've all probably heard of Michael Jordan, whether or not we have any interest in basketball. He's recognized as one of the most talented athletes of all time, has broken all sorts of records in his sport, and has earned an income most of us will only ever dream of. Did you know that when he was interviewed, and asked what was the most significant moment of his life, he answered that it was the time he was dropped from his high school team? It wasn't all the fame, power, and amazing achievements of his life, but the fact he was dropped from his high school team. This, he said, gave him time to focus and to practice—and gave him more determination than ever to become great.

Even with all this greatness, and being known as one of the greatest athletes of all time, his switch to professional baseball was at best average and at worst forgettable. Even he discovered: You cannot be a jack-of-all-trades, no matter how talented.

Great rewards come from clear focus. When you focus all your effort, energy, and attention in one direction, you can become truly outstanding in that area. This will not only give you the best result, it will allow you to move more quickly to the next thing and do it well.

Great rewards come from clear focus.

When I started Vision Publishing, I was focused on one thing—creating and selling business book summaries. That meant I couldn't create a direct mail business, or seminars, or any other business. But when the summaries started to succeed because of my focus on them, I found I could build Vision Publishing into a business with hundreds of products. My options exploded when I succeeded in that one thing.

When you focus and succeed, you have a wider range of life choices—I've sold my interest in Vision Publishing, so now I can refocus on whatever I want. I have complete freedom in how I spend my time, who I work with, and what business I do. That freedom came from focus.

Without focus, being a jack-of-all-trades, you're destined to be average. Average means taking the seemingly safe route, always hedging your bets, never standing out, and never being offered anything special. Being average at what you do means you'll never have anything other than an average life.

I have seen many business owners who are trying to do too many things at once. They've had spectacular results after I have pointed this out and they've refocused on one activity. Which activity you choose depends on your dreams, the price you're willing to pay, and exactly what you want from work. But if we're talking about business success, usually your best option is to focus on the activity that brings the biggest financial result in the shortest possible time.

CHAPTER 11

How to Get Everything You Want in Life

One of Australia's most common products is the Post-it Note, manufactured by 3M. It was developed because of two people's creativity and a company's positive attitude.

A 3M researcher was doing a bit of "experimental doodling" and came up with a glue that he thought was a complete dud. It stuck to paper, but not very well. Another 3M worker had a problem marking songs in his choir book and came up with the idea of adhesive bookmarks. When the two got together, the company supported them and a great product was born. The only reason it happened was because 3M encouraged its people to come up with creative solutions and was positive about the ideas its people produced.

Creativity and a positive attitude can have similar effects in your life and business. Quite often a single creative thought is all you need to get what you want in life. Creative thoughts aren't exclusive to rich and successful people. The key is to accept that you are as smart as anyone else and just as capable of good ideas. Demand the best ideas from yourself and from others. All the time.

This means that you have to be willing to kick it around, to take risks with your ideas, and to support people who come to you with new ideas. Some of them will be terrible. Some will be great. Be gentle with yourself and others— don't judge people on whether their ideas are good or bad, but congratulate them for their creativity. You never know where the next great idea is coming from.

The only thing stopping you from displaying your creative genius is your own self-doubt and your own judgments about the ideas you come up with.

You Can Change Your Life with a Single Thought!

Your own thoughts are the most powerful influence in your life. Your thoughts *are you,* so the more negative and self-defeating thoughts you have, the less successful you'll be.

Quite often a single creative thought is all you need to get what you want in life.

It's easy to say "Be a positive thinker," but for many people it's not natural or easy to do. Willpower alone won't help you do this. Your mind always has to contain something—that's just the way it is. You can't just empty your mind of negative thoughts. You need to replace them with positive messages.

History is filled with stories of people who have succeeded after years of failure. These people had faith in what they were doing despite failing and being attacked by those who doubted. What keeps all achievers going is their optimistic faith in what they believe they can do, not focusing on what they cannot do or control.

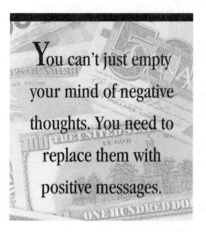

You can't just empty your mind of negative thoughts. You need to replace them with positive messages.

Wayne Dyer and Robert Seligman are two writers who can teach us a lot about optimism and vision. In his book, *Learned Optimism,* Seligman connects being optimistic with a whole range of success in business and in life. He shows how optimists are more successful, more healthy, and have better relationships than people who view the world negatively. The single most important thing I have taken from his book is that if you can learn to be optimistic, you increase your chances of success a hundredfold.

Dyer's book, *You'll Believe It When You See It,* doesn't talk directly about optimism. But it talks about the power of vision, and of making a vision of your future. Dyer shows how a vision can help bring about a reality. Building a positive, optimistic picture in your mind helps you get to where you want to be.

Where most people go wrong is in being mistakenly led to believe that they can wake up one day and through sheer will and determination become an optimist. This is completely incorrect. Willpower on its own is insufficient.

Dan S. Kennedy, in his book *How to Succeed in Business by Breaking All the Rules,* says that you can think positively all you like, yet negative things will still happen to you. You will get caught in traffic, you will spill coffee on your new outfit, you will lose a sale, and you will get cheated or be disappointed from time to time. Authors Anthony Robbins and W. Mitchell advise that being positive is not about creating a positive expectancy through willpower. Rather, it's about taking personal power and raising self-esteem through controlling, not the outcome of an event, but the way you respond to that outcome.

In other words, they say being positive is about understanding that sometimes you'll be given a lemon, and positive thinking begins and ends with your initiative in turning that lemon into lemonade.

Dr. Maxwell Maltz, author of *Psycho-Cybernetics,* which has sold more than 30 million copies, said that no amount of conscious positive thinking will overcome a negative self-image. Positive thinking is directly linked to what a person believes she can and cannot do. From this we can say that positive thinking comes from taking positive action to overcome any event you see as being negative. If you do this frequently enough, this positive pattern becomes a habit over time. This is how positive mental attitudes develop.

If you understand that you have control of your actions and reactions, you not only get better results, but you also have a much better journey through life. Isn't it better to go through life with the knowledge and belief that you are not a victim of circumstance but are in control of your choices?

HOW SOME NEGATIVE THINKING
WILL MAKE YOU RICH

It is a widely held belief that filling your mind with positive thoughts can spur you into action. You need only to consider the huge number of books, tapes, and seminars on the subject to appreciate how thoroughly this concept has been documented, analyzed, and marketed. Over the years, positive thinking has been credited with many people's success, especially those who overcame terrible hardship. Within this positive-thinking culture, negative thinking is often thought of as the enemy of success. However, this is not the only way of looking at it.

It is just as important to consider negative thinking as useful in business and in life because ignoring negative thoughts may mean you are not being realistic about what you are attempting to achieve. Having a balanced view means being positive but taking into account the negative side of things as well. Then you can approach a challenge well prepared; for example, by anticipating all the pitfalls. Negative thinking ensures you have considered everything that may go wrong and positive thinking will motivate you to overcome those issues. This is why negative thinking can actually be a good thing.

You Need Something Far More Valuable Than Money Before You Get Rich

Your personal values—what you think is right and wrong—are the bedrock of your success. I've emphasized that success isn't just about money; it's about what's important to you, and about being consistent about what's important to you. Doing well in one area of your life, while sacrificing your values in another, is not success.

Having unbreakable values gives you a real sense of worth, because you've set your standards and met them, and you know that you'll keep on meeting them. These can be personal moral standards, business ethics, or the standards you set for your staff.

Having no committed values, or values you bend when it suits you, will undermine whatever you achieve. If you can't look at yourself and feel you are the sort of person you want to be, what difference will money, sex, or fame make?

Bending your values will make you feel worthless, destroy your confidence, and eat at your self-esteem. Don't sell out for anybody or any amount of money. If your values are strong enough, real success will come.

Be patient, select values that are fair and true, and stick to those values like glue. In the long term the rightness of your values will give you personal strength and your business commercial strength—the strengths that breed success.

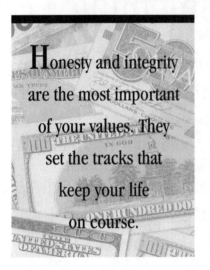

Honesty and integrity are the most important of your values. They set the tracks that keep your life on course.

ONE THING MONEY CANNOT REPLACE ONCE YOU'VE LOST IT

If you've been in business a while, you'll know that honesty and integrity on their own won't make you rich. Without them, however, you may find your success short-lived or empty, if you manage to get there at all.

Honesty and integrity are the most important of your values. They set the tracks that keep your life on course. A life lived honestly is a life lived without fear or bad conscience, because you live knowing that you do what you think is right.

Just about anything else you lose can be replaced—money, buildings, equipment—whole companies even. But your name, reputation, and conscience, once ruined, can never be repaired. You have to live with that forever.

THE VISION VALUES STATEMENT

When I set up Vision Publishing, one of the first things I did was establish clear values and make sure we lived by them everyday. The statement below was given to every staff member and was posted in clear view in every work area:

Members of the Vision team are expected to understand and to work by our values, which we hope will become your personal values too:

- We are honest in our dealings
- We work hard for fair rewards
- We are fair and thoughtful
- We give before we get in life
- We seek to understand the other person before needing to be understood ourselves
- We are proactive, not reactive
- We strive to learn something new everyday
- We offer a constructive solution when we complain
- We are not afraid to make mistakes and learn from them
- We correct our mistakes and learn from them
- We make a commitment to our work and ourselves
- We take responsibility for our results and our own future
- We set clear goals before beginning a task
- We choose to over-communicate rather than under-communicate
- We ask good questions of ourselves and others to get good answers
- We know our future rewards and successes are directly linked to the actions and commitments we make today.

It may mean that you end up with less money in the short term. It may mean making tough decisions, but it will always be worth it. If you're honest with others and with yourself, your decisions will always be right. They'll be decisions that will build strong relationships with the people who ultimately make you successful—your customers.

Honesty starts with complete congruency between what you say and what you do. Your word must be your bond. If you make this one of your unbreakable rules, people will trust you. In the long term, trust and your good name are worth everything. They will build your business, will bring you customers, and will make your reputation valuable. Your life and business will only get easier, as people recommend you and give you new and unexpected opportunities—because they want to do business with people they trust.

THEY'LL SEE THROUGH YOU

Integrity is one thing you can't pretend to have. Sooner or later you'll get caught and the word will spread. Even if you aren't caught, though, dishonesty will eat at you from the inside.

This is especially true when you try to be selectively honest. You know the type: Honest to those who are important or rich and a double-dealing liar to people they think don't count. They're out there, and they make money, but they leave a trail behind them that smells a little off.

It isn't smart business, and it's not living within values that will build your long-term success. Real success comes when you treat everyone as valuable and worthy of your attention. No matter who customers are, eventually they'll see through any insincerity. And more importantly, you'll know that you aren't living your values. Any behavior like that undermines all your relationships and any happiness you find in your life. You can't separate what you do at work from how you live your life.

You Get Rich by Helping Others Get What They Want First

Become obsessed with serving others, but remember that "service" does not mean "subservience." Often we get these two confused. It should be an honor to provide genuine service to someone else. The Japanese certainly think so, and their attitude has taken them from financial disaster just fifty years ago to becoming one of the world's most powerful economies.

Serving others is about finding a way to help answer their needs and interests. It's about helping people achieve what they want. It could be a small step such as getting the food they want, or something bigger such as getting the house they want. When you focus on doing what you can to help others get what they want, you will have discovered one of the greatest secrets to success.

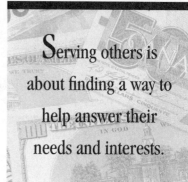

Serving others is about finding a way to help answer their needs and interests.

This idea has been around for a long time; you may have heard it in any customer service course. You may also have encountered it in Stephen Covey's *The Seven Habits of Highly Successful People.* I learned this from my father, who sold electrical goods in the sixties and seventies. Often he would get a call from a customer on a Sunday because something wasn't working. He and I would set off immediately to go and correct the situation. His whole focus was, "They're my customers and my friends, why wouldn't I want to help them?" And every one of those visits was free of charge. With that sort of ethic you can't go wrong.

GIVE OR GET—ONE THING THE RICH KNOW

"Giving" suggests you'll end up with less, but the laws of nature ensure you'll end up with more. Many people still don't understand this. Even those who do understand it misuse it, or don't use it enough. This is strange, because as a principle, it's ancient—it's even taught in the Bible.

In every situation you can always look for what's in it for you. That's the shark style of doing business. Alternatively, you can look for what's in it for somebody else. I believe that in business, and in relationships, we can get much further if we always look to give to others first. This may seem a strange concept to many, but it actually works.

Giving honestly will always bring unexpected pleasures that money just cannot buy.

I know of two consultants who do their business very differently. Adam is a good salesman who goes in, gives the client a standard solution whether it's 100 percent right or not, and gets out with lots of cash. Chris, on the other hand, spends a lot of time finding out what the problem is so he can really understand it. He'll challenge the client and try to give them not only what they want but something that will help them, even if he can't charge for it. Adam makes one quick sale. Chris makes a customer for life.

Giving builds trust and relationships that turn one-time prospects into loyal customers, but giving is about more than building business. It's a way of being in the world; it's about being a decent person.

Try it for a while and see if I'm right. Giving doesn't necessarily mean giving money to charity. It can mean giving your time or energy to your partner, friends, or kids. It can be doing something nice for a complete stranger. Something as cheap as a smile or a compliment can bring joy to somebody else and cost you very little. Do it, but only do it if you genuinely mean it—if you have other motives it will show through. Giving honestly will always bring unexpected pleasures that money just cannot buy.

Passion Is the Secret Weapon of the Rich

Success is rarely, if ever, an overnight phenomenon. What you see as a success is invariably the result of years of effort, of failures and restarts, of hurdles cleared and problems avoided. The only things that can fuel such a long drive to success are passion and commitment.

Most people are passionate when they first venture into business, when the excitement is electric and the dream of freedom is vivid. But in most cases, business reality sets in within a year, and it turns out to be hard, stressful work. People get swamped. They don't focus on what's important; they don't treat themselves and their staff in the right way. It's then that the worst—or the best—in people appears, depending on the strength of their Personal Foundations (see page 37). For many, the passion starts to disappear, usually because they lack basic skills to make their business work.

As the passion recedes, it's replaced by fear, doubt, worry, and visions of disaster. A salaried, stress-free job starts to look pretty good after all. People start operating in survival mode, struggling to keep the business afloat—short of capital, short of customers, short of time, and short of personal satisfaction.

Once you're at this stage, you can't manage a business, think clearly, see opportunities, or motivate and lead your staff. Once you lose the passion, the death knell has sounded. Unless the passion can be reborn, it's just a matter of time before the doors are closed for good or the liquidator steps in.

If you've lost the passion, you've lost the game. You've got to take steps to keep your passion alive—by making sure you love what you do.

DO THE RICH DO WHAT THEY LOVE, OR LOVE WHAT THEY DO?

This challenge is foolproof. Find any rich or successful person and I'll show you a person who absolutely loves what he does. It is impossible to achieve long-term success unless you love doing whatever it is you do. Every rich, famous, or successful person I have encountered says exactly the same thing—whether I have interviewed them, read about them, or listened to them. They would happily pay to do what others pay them to do. They all find it quite amusing that they get paid to do a job that they would do for nothing.

If you don't absolutely love what you do, if you are not in love with your customers, if Monday mornings are not a positive experience for you, perhaps you're in the wrong business.

If you love what you're doing, it's obvious and it's infectious. But when you're just going through the motions,

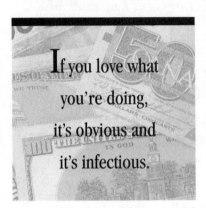

If you love what you're doing, it's obvious and it's infectious.

people notice the minute the passion is not there. If you're flat and have no energy, it flows to your staff, to your customers, and to your profit.

Not every day can be an over-the-top fun day. We all experience daily problems and crises, but if you aren't inspired to make a difference, then you're in the wrong place. When you don't get a kick out of serving your customers well, or from helping your staff to grow and achieve, you aren't enjoying the things that are essential to business success.

Life rewards excellence. You will never be excellent or rich unless you absolutely, passionately love what you are doing.

I have a question for you. You have only one life: Why would you want to spend a minute of it doing something you don't love doing?

DON'T BE AFRAID TO ABANDON SHIP AND TAKE A LONG SWIM

When the passion is gone and the excitement has deserted you, you have to ask yourself if you're in the right place. If the answer is yes, then you have to recommit and rediscover that passion. But if it is no, don't be afraid to give up what you are to become what you might be.

At his seminars, real estate wizard John McGrath asks his audience what their level of excitement and passion is for their business. The scale is from 1 to 10, with 10 meaning that you are totally consumed and loving every minute of it and 1 meaning that you barely register a pulse beat. Usually, most of his audience rate themselves around 5 or 6. That's incredible!

This means most people accept mediocrity from themselves and from their lives. This is why most people go through life earning average money and being aversely happy. It's the 8s, 9s, and 10s who end up with the majority—the ones with the excitement and passion for what they do.

P COMES IMMEDIATELY BEFORE C IN A RICH PERSON'S ALPHABET

Passion is meaningless without commitment. Commitment is what takes a passionate dream and makes it real. It drives you to keep going despite the barriers in your way. Above all else, commitment means accepting what you have to do to reach your dream.

In life, anything worthwhile comes with a price. Paying the price means paying your dues in time, sweat, tears, and discipline. Author Jim Rohn points out that we all must suffer from one of two pains—the pain of discipline or the pain of regret. We must suffer the pain of discipline to

Above all else, commitment means accepting what you have to do to reach your dream.

achieve what we want or the pain of regret at not achieving it. The difference is that the pain of discipline weighs ounces, while the pain of regret weighs tons.

Take yourself forward to the end of your life and imagine yourself with that weight of regret. It's not a pleasant thought. All it takes to shift that weight is some discipline and commitment now. The good news is that discipline will also make your dreams real—and make them real now.

PAY BEFORE YOU ENTER

To be successful, at some point you will need to work long and hard. This doesn't mean that you must spend your whole life working. Balance is equally important, or life will have no meaning. When you're aiming at success, however, eight hours a day is just for survival. More is where success begins. Being committed means being prepared to do whatever it takes—while also having the ability to enjoy the journey.

Being committed means being prepared to do whatever it takes—while also having the ability to enjoy the journey.

Look at any sports star. On nearly every occasion you will see that near-perfect swing, that reliably brilliant performance, but what you never see are the months, years, and even decades of practice dedicated to achieving this—before you or anyone else ever heard of him. He's paid the price in advance.

This doesn't just apply to business successes and sports stars. It goes with being a great teacher, a great musician, a great parent—anything. I know one of the leading immunologists in Sydney—or at least she was. She decided to pay the price for being the parent that she wanted to be. She sacrificed a huge income, a prestigious career, and the benefits of years of training and an assured future so she could look after her child. She decided what she wanted and committed herself to it, no matter what the cost. Now she's a success as the sort of mother she wanted to be.

There's a price for everything. You need to find out what it is, then pay it up front and in full.

PERSIST AND PROSPER

Life's way of testing your true beliefs is to make things difficult. There were many occasions when I felt like giving up. Years ago, when I was looking for a job, I reached a state of despair and thought I was beaten. I had no money, no way of paying debts, and few paying customers. I was eating plain rice because it was all I could afford.

The only thing you can do is persist. Once you have made the decision to persist, and you reach the other side, simply pushing through a difficulty is never as bad as it seemed at the time.

Although persistence is critical, however, there is a bit more to it than simply persisting. You've probably heard the saying: "If at first you don't succeed, try, try again." This is all well and good and of course you should never give up on your dreams, but if you know something just isn't working it's vital to stop doing it and try a new approach. Persistence is important for success but it's essential to be open-minded and flexible in how you set about achieving it.

> **P**ersistence is important for success but it's essential to be open-minded and flexible in how you set about achieving it.

If you try something and it doesn't work, *don't* try again until you have figured out why you failed.

No doubt you've heard the story of Thomas Edison, who tried thousands of times to invent a lightbulb. Napoleon Hill, author of *Think and Grow Rich,* asked him what he would be doing now if his ten-thousandth experiment had failed. Edison replied: "I would not be standing here talking to you; I would be in my laboratory conducting the next experiment."

Edison did not talk of conducting the *same* experiment again. He didn't do the same experiment over and over and hope that it would work next time. Rather, he learned from his mistakes and then tried a different tack. This sounds obvious, but in many cases people just don't do it. They go on and on doing the same thing, expecting a different result. This is a major reason why people never achieve their dreams and simply give up.

CHAPTER 14

Rich People Feel Alive and Exhilarated Because of Risk

Most people avoid risk like the plague. They see it as something bad. Rich people don't. In fact, they thrive on it.

Can you remember the rush you felt stepping off a roller coaster after a ride you just took? Do you remember how it made you feel? Excited, exhilarated, alive, wanting to do more of it? Successful people get the same rush when they face risk. They make a conscious decision to overcome their fear, accept responsibility, and win. When this occurs the rush is incredible. It gives life a whole new dimension—one that most people will never experience. Facing and accepting risk gives you a sense of purpose and a set of feelings you simply cannot describe, and it spurs you on to find that next rush.

In the story of *Braveheart,* when William Wallace was urging his underweaponed, undertrained band of courageous Scots to attack against overwhelming odds, he said:

"Listen . . . all men eventually die . . . but some men never really live!" If you stop to ponder this, it is indisputably true.

Go out there and live, have fun, take risks, get excited—you'll be surprised to see what happens to your life when you take this approach.

CHAPTER 15

Take Responsibility and Take Charge

When you accept responsibility for your life and your actions, you're taking charge and making things happen, rather than waiting for someone else to do it for you. This will usually involve a risk: some commitment from you.

This principle applies whether you are self-employed or you work for someone else. You must work with the fervor and responsibility you would adopt in your own business. Everyone will benefit—most of all you.

Having this mentality, whether you're in your own business or a salaried job, gives you self-worth, respect, and a power to determine your own path. Too many people do not understand how powerful this is and what a difference it can make to their lives.

The Rich Are the Biggest Failures

How can the rich be the biggest failures? Siimon Reynolds, one of Australia's most successful and influential advertising gurus, has said many times that successful people fail more than failures. But he then goes on to say that rich and successful people are different from failures in one respect: They keep learning and working toward their goals until eventually they succeed.

Successful people expect to fail, but do not see it as a bad or negative experience. They also realize that history is no reflection of the future. They know that, if you have failed in the past, this doesn't mean you will necessarily fail in the future. On the other hand, they know that previous success does not guarantee you continued success. You need to keep working on it.

It isn't just the business cycle that goes up and down. There are always problems and successes in your business, your life, your relationships, and everything else that matters to you. Things change, problems arise, people leave. All this means is that you have to deal with difficulties every day of your life.

How you decide to view and deal with these setbacks is one thing that will separate you from the ones who truly fail. How do you cope with the stress and anxiety that hit when things are not going your way? How do you stay committed and focused enough to find the answers and keep going?

It's tough, but it's essential that you do. By continuing, you give yourself the chance to reach the success you aimed for—quit and you never will.

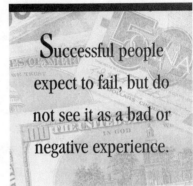

Successful people expect to fail, but do not see it as a bad or negative experience.

Every successful person has had ups and downs. They may be due to cash flow, changes in the market, a competitor's moves, or the loss of key employees. Business is about risk and change, so tough times are always just around the corner.

If you know this, and expect it, it becomes easier to take short-term failure in your stride, put it in perspective, and learn from it. The cycle will eventually turn around. When it does, you'll know more and be stronger than before.

TAKE A DIFFERENT LOOK AT WHAT GOES WRONG

You can transform the way you experience your failure by shifting your perspective.

People believe the grass is always greener on the other side of the fence. This isn't true. If it is greener it's usually only because there's more stinking cow dung over there.

Don't punish yourself; you haven't picked the toughest industry, and everyone else isn't doing it easier than you. You simply don't see what goes on beneath that layer of green grass—where the manure, the dirt, and the mess are doing their job. Everyone's paying a price, and the greener the grass, the higher the price people have paid. That price includes failure.

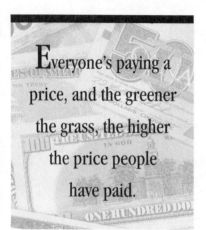

Everyone's paying a price, and the greener the grass, the higher the price people have paid.

If you wallow in your failure (and we all do it sometimes), change your focus and spend a moment contemplating the problems of other people in the world. You'll suddenly realize that what seemed catastrophic for you doesn't compare with others' problems. Focus on someone else's problem, work with them, and help them to solve it, and you'll get a great sense of what's positive about where you are and where you can go.

You can also create this mental transformation by looking at what you've achieved to get to where you are. You must have done something right to get this far. Stop and reflect on what you've done and give yourself a small pat on the back. Everyone's history is full of great solutions to difficult problems—we just forget to see it that way. In difficult times, review your past and draw strength from all those creative decisions you made. It will instantly reduce some of the stress and anxiety and give you confidence in your ability to come out on top.

When a problem is taking over your life, try to distance yourself from it for a while. Catch a movie, play a round of golf, go for a run—it doesn't matter what it is, but do something different. Time out is very important, not only for giving you some balance in your life, but also for finding buried solutions to difficult problems. Often the breathing space gives your unconscious mind the chance to work on the solution. Many successful people will tell you their biggest breakthroughs came while they were in the shower or walking the dog. "Sleep on it" sounds like a cliché, but it can be a very effective way to reach an answer.

FAILURE—YOUR GREATEST FRIEND

Failure is there to make us better, wiser, smarter, more cautious, or even more adventurous. Be realistic about failure and you'll see that it is a tremendous opportunity.

You can even become excited about it! Failing gives you the information you need to do better. Most acts of genius come after years of trying to solve a problem and failing. The great minds and scientists of history often spent most of their lives failing. Yet their ability to learn from their failures has literally created the world we live in today.

Science is full of these stories. Friedrich Kekule discovered benzene, one of the building blocks of modern chemistry, after seven years of failing. He persisted and ultimately saw in a dream what looked like a snake eating its tail. With that dream he realized that benzene was actually a ring. For

Kekule, and for many other geniuses, it was his failure that allowed him to make the step to success.

So how do you make failure your greatest friend? If your back is in a corner, you have no choice but to fight your way out. When you're confronted by failure, you have to act. It's usually at these times you will find breakthrough solutions you would never have considered otherwise.

Failure is a wonderful catalyst for change. Few of us love change for change's sake; usually we have to be prodded to accept it. The discomfort of failure and desperate times—the dry mouth, the anxiety, the knot in the stomach—is our motivation to accept and embrace change. Stepping out of our comfort zone to deal with a problem is an important step to success.

CHAPTER

Move Fast or Get Out of the Way

If you become a master at your trade, you will be able to do it better and quicker than anyone else, and this will build your reputation. Get a reputation for speed and urgency, and you'll be amazed how it will repay you.

Moving fast allows you to take opportunities you might otherwise miss, it minimizes the costs of ongoing problems, and it instills passion and urgency in your staff. But it is more than a nice extra. It is essential, because if you don't act quickly on things that matter, your customers will go somewhere else and your life and business will stagnate. If you have to do something, do it now. If it needs doing tomorrow, do it today. And then get onto the next task.

In business you have to decide fast as well as act fast. Making decisions for some people is worse than having a tooth pulled, but from my experience, you're better off making a decision—taking the risk of making the wrong one— than procrastinating or not making a decision at all.

The most successful people make lightning-fast decisions involving millions of dollars. To an observer they may seem irresponsible, because it doesn't seem to be a "considered" decision. These successful people realize, however, that noth-

If you have to do something, do it now. If it needs doing tomorrow, do it today.

ing in life is perfect and that you may have to make a decision based on limited or imperfect information. Dithering will only make things more risky, not less.

With the benefit of hindsight, you may discover that your decision turned out to be the wrong one. Many decisions are. But most decisions help you move forward to a new vantage point. Even if your decision was wrong, chances are that you'll be in a better position than if you had done nothing.

STAGE FRIGHT WON'T EMBARRASS YOU—IT'LL BANKRUPT YOU

At some stage in business you may find you freeze, are unable to make a decision, and feel afraid of where you're going. This is what I call stage fright, and it's very common. It usually appears at the time when success is just around the corner or when changes are coming.

When you operate out of fear, you can't practice your Personal Foundations (see page 37). Fear changes how you operate and how your business operates. The normal reaction is to "batten down the hatches"—both for the business and for the individual. This is an attitude of no-risk, no-change, no-future. People lose their optimism and positive attitude, and lose sight of the dream that is driving them.

Although this is a natural reaction, it isn't one that will lead you to success. You must act fast to move forward, but if you're not competent in business, the action you choose may well be the wrong one. This could trap you and contribute even more to your stage fright.

The only reason you're trapped is because you don't know what the right action is. This means that first you must find the knowledge you need to act, and then learn it quickly. It might mean learning under pressure, but learning under pressure is better than doing nothing. It forces you to set learning and business goals with an uncompromising time limit. Taking positive action and making better decisions are what it's all about. If that means you've got to learn something fast, so be it.

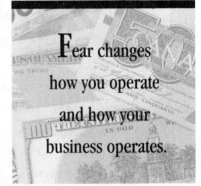

Fear changes how you operate and how your business operates.

When I was managing Vision Publishing, I had this very experience. I had to make quick decisions about short-term financing, printing options, and personnel problems. When I started the business I knew little about these things. The important thing is to read up on what you can, ask the experts, and learn from them. Then decide and act, even if you're not sure. Deciding without being sure is often what entrepreneurs have to do.

Always, Always Be Self-Employed

No matter where you are in life and whatever you are doing, whether you are starting in the mail room and earning minimum wage or are an executive of a large firm, you should never ever think of yourself as just an employee. The most successful people in life are those who see themselves as their own small business.

When you do this, you will find ways to make your work more enjoyable and more fun, and you will become more efficient. You will arrive a little earlier, leave a little later, and produce better quality work without it being an effort.

Others, especially your employers, will notice the difference between you and your co-workers, and when it comes time for a raise, promotion, or special project, you will be first on the list. If you find this difficult, it's probably because you are in the wrong job.

To become rich, however, your long-term goal is to become self-employed, owning and operating your own business. Having this mentality before you embark on this is important, because without it you are going to find the transition very difficult.

If You Are Still Skeptical, Just Ask Jerry

If you still have doubts about the power of Personal Foundations (see page 37) and their enormous role in gaining you riches, just ask Jerry Seinfeld.

We all now know the worldwide success of his TV sitcom, *Seinfeld,* which made Jerry an international star and multimillionaire. But what most people don't know is that Jerry was considered among his peers as "average." He had done the club circuit for more than ten years, his career going nowhere.

His attempt to lift himself above the pack, by approaching NBC to do a sitcom pilot, was met with indifference. After much persistence on his part they agreed, due to a shortage of upcoming sitcoms, and funded the smallest pilot in history, allowing just four shows to be produced.

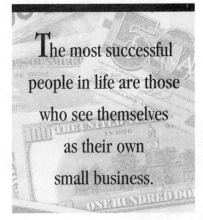

The most successful people in life are those who see themselves as their own small business.

Test audiences also gave it the thumbs down, commenting that his show was weak with a low-quality cast. It even started off slow in the ratings department, but its timing, directly after the hot sitcom *Cheers,* weaned people onto the show. Ratings started going through the roof, and *Seinfeld* gained cult status among a broad range of viewers. To this day, Seinfeld keeps the "bad" NBC research report framed and on the wall in his lavish home to remind him of the fine line between success and failure and his amazing success in the face of all the negative feelings, opinions, and evidence of others.

PART THREE

Your Marketing

The Machine That Drives Your Business

Marketing is the second critical area of your business. It's the machine that drives your business—the skill that makes or breaks you. Why? Because, when used correctly, marketing can be the biggest profit-making tool you will find in business.

Consider this: A client had a single advertisement written, planned, and placed for $5,000. It brought $10,000 worth of business and the client was happy to make a profit. We wrote a similar ad for him, of the same size and at the same cost, that brought $50,000 worth of business.

With the same time, effort, and money, one business can be as much as five times more successful than another. All because of superior marketing. That superior marketing comes about only when you really understand what marketing is—which is something very few people do.

What I've learned, and the best definition that I've heard, is: Marketing is focusing on your customers' needs rather than on your product or service—and profit is the by-product.

Successful, skillful marketing is the key that builds your business into the success you want it to be. Ignore it at your peril.

MARKETING IS TOO IMPORTANT TO LEAVE TO THE MARKETING PEOPLE

Even though marketing is a key tool for business success, many business owners and CEOs still delegate the marketing responsibility.

The CEO of Hewlett Packard once said, "Marketing is too important to leave to the marketing people." There isn't a truer statement. Marketing and hiring key staff are two business functions that should never, on any account, be reduced in importance or delegated to anyone lower in an organization than the CEO. CEOs need to be completely involved and on top of them. That doesn't mean they have to actually do the marketing work, but they need to understand *everything* about what's going on. And it has to be completely clear and make sense.

HOW TO CUT THROUGH THE MARKETING "DOUBLE-TALK"

Because marketing is so important to your success, you must at all times understand exactly what is going on. Don't let marketing jargon or double-talk impress you or make you feel inadequate, and never feel you should leave this issue to the experts. Ask good questions, dig deep, and discover the answers for yourself.

Look at your marketing campaign and strategy. Put yourself completely into your customer's shoes, use your common sense, and see if you would respond to your own advertisements or promotions. If your answer is "probably not," then the bad news is: neither will your customers. If you can't clearly see how the strategy or campaign will sell, dump it! If your marketing effort does not bring a new customer to your business and generate a sale, then it's a waste of money.

Marketing is focusing on your customers' needs rather than on your product or service—and profit is the by-product.

You can easily judge your marketing because the most important aspect of it is common sense. Good marketing focuses on your customers and treats them as normal people. People want value, fun, excitement, honesty, fairness—and not necessarily the cheapest prices. They want to be treated with care and respect, and as individuals. They don't want to take risks in dealing with you, and they don't want it to be hard to do business with you. They want to be treated as a friend. All this is simple common sense.

Think about it: If you wanted to invite friends over for a party, would you run a boring ad or send them impersonal letters they wouldn't even read? This might sound ridiculous, but this is precisely what most businesses do—and still expect people to respond to them.

Unless you're very lucky, if you give up the responsibility for marketing in your business, your business will end up in the toilet.

BEST PRODUCT IS NOT ALWAYS THE BEST

Can't you succeed in business by simply having the *best* product or service? The answer is both yes—and no.

Not every business can have the best product or service. Not everyone gets to sell Rolls-Royces or Cartier watches.

What you must realize is that you need the *best* product or service suited *for your market*. Not everybody can afford a Rolls-Royce, but there are plenty of people looking for a good, reasonably priced Nissan or Saturn.

What you must realize is that you need the best product or service suited for your market.

When you choose a product for your business, you need to be sure there is a big enough market for it. If only you and your friends are going to buy it, you're not going to get rich selling it. Be careful about what you choose, look at the market, do your research, and watch the trends.

Be careful not to select or develop products or services that are ahead of their time or their market, unless you have very deep pockets. This is a surefire way to go broke—waiting for your product or service to catch on.

On the other hand, the same danger awaits if you try to get in when the market is on the decline. You may be caught with too much stock and too few customers. This is a real danger today, as customer choices and markets change so rapidly.

As obvious as this sounds, it is not always the best product or service that is the winner. What sells best is the product or service that appeals best to the most buyers in a market. And that depends a lot on your marketing skill, not your product.

CHOOSE YOUR PRODUCT VERY CAREFULLY

Even if you feel your timing is right to launch a product or service, you must be aware of the possible high cost of educating the market about it.

Launching a new or improved version of an existing product requires far less customer education than if you are offering a new product concept. With new concept launches, it sometimes take years and millions of dollars to educate the market.

Your payback period will not be quick, and you may run out of resources to eventually cash in. Even if you do make it through this treacherous and costly period, you will find, as soon as the market starts to respond positively, that your returns will be eroded by competition stepping in to take advantage of the prime market opportunity.

Everyday items we now take for granted often took years to be accepted by the market. For example, it was thirteen years before people began to understand and become comfortable with microwave ovens. Many companies went broke during this period.

Note that inventors are not usually the ones who end up rich. It is almost always the entrepreneur who picks up the concept when the timing is right and makes the product successful. Take McDonald's as another example. If it weren't for Ray Kroc's entrepreneurial zeal, there would be no McDonald's as we know it today. The original McDonald brothers were happy with one store.

Does this mean that, if the timing is right, market education is not necessary? Certainly not! In order to be successful, you need to constantly educate your market. There

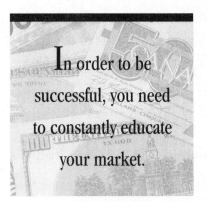

is, however, a big cost difference between educating your market about a new concept and educating your customers about what is unique about you and why they should buy from you as opposed to someone else.

In order to be successful, you need to constantly educate your market.

If you are offering a product or service that is already understood, or not difficult to understand, then your goal must be to educate your customers about why they should buy from you. This means giving them solid and plausible reasons why they should select you or your company to do business with. This important educational tool is called a Unique Selling Proposition (USP). You can see this in the ongoing campaigns from market leaders such as Coca-Cola, McDonald's, Levis, and others. They're way ahead as market leaders, yet they still spend millions on educating their market.

The message for now is to realize simply that customer education is part of running a successful business. The cost can't be too high, however, because if it is, something must be wrong with your product or service, your message, or your market timing.

In marketing a new product, you need to select it carefully. Although a product may be new and exciting to you, this does not automatically make it a winner. The risks are high. It is usually better to market a product that is well known to consumers yet is new and improved by you. This is a safer route for you, especially if you do not have an unlimited budget for marketing and promotion.

What Is Marketing?

I've emphasized many things in this book, but none more important than the fact that marketing is focusing on your customers' needs rather than on your product or service.

What's interesting to you (your product, your business, your people, and your processes) is irrelevant to the customer. What they want is something that answers their needs, not yours. That's what marketing is about: identifying, addressing, and answering customer needs. Always be prepared to put yourself in your customers' shoes and to make sure satisfying their needs is what your business is doing.

Good marketing means having the ability to change your point of view so that you always:

$ Understand your customer
$ Empathize with your customer
$ Relate to your customer
$ Love your customer

$ Help your customer in every way

$ Contribute to your customer's life

$ Add value to every transaction

YOU'RE PROBABLY IN THE WRONG BUSINESS!

Forget what business you are in—it's irrelevant. Forget what product you're selling—it's irrelevant too. None of us are in the product or service business. We're all in the people business because people are the ones who make decisions and spend money. And when we're in the people business, we're also in the problem-solving business—solving people's problems.

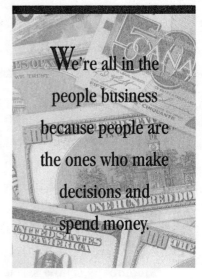

We're all in the people business because people are the ones who make decisions and spend money.

To become rich, you must become a master of recognizing people's needs and desires, and of finding ways to satisfy them. If you can consistently do that quicker, cheaper, better, more conveniently, and with more trustworthiness and honesty than anyone else, you can't help but make a lot of money.

If you focus on the customer in all the ways I've listed, you'll have greater insight into what they really need or desire and what problems they have that you can help fix. From this knowledge you can go about applying your technical skill and expertise to provide them with a unique solution that will sell, and sell well.

MARKETING EVEN THE RICH
KNOW HOW TO DO

When you know what customers like and don't like, what they read and don't read, where they live, and what they do for a living or for fun, your business is on sure ground. This intimate knowledge allows you to communicate with them and serve them in the way they want.

Customer intimacy may seem like hard work, but if you don't do it up front you'll never really know who your real customer is. Sometimes this isn't obvious because the user and buyer may be two different people. If you don't do this work up front, you'll be forced to do it later on. Why? Because you will have wasted time and thousands of dollars on inaccurate strategies, ineffective marketing, and damaging advertising campaigns.

If you get your marketing messages wrong, it takes a lot of work to get them back on track. Remember what happened with the new formula Coca-Cola? The company tried to force it on a market whose desire was for the old taste. The formula bombed and the company lost millions.

Selling Office Space

A company selling serviced office space wanted to increase their occupancy rates. They used to run yellow pages advertising and business press advertisements. Both cost many thousands of dollars.

When a potential customer would call, they'd ask about the cost of the space. The company would give the prices over the phone, and in a desperate hope to get a sale would ask if they could send out a brochure. One in thirty callers would call back.

By putting themselves in their customers' shoes, and by doing a little research, the company realized that people cannot buy office space over the phone or from a brochure.

They scrapped the expensive brochures and replaced them with a classy invitation to come in and visit, which cost less than a quarter of the price. From then on, when a call came, no prices were given over the phone and the customer was invited to make an appointment and visit the offices.

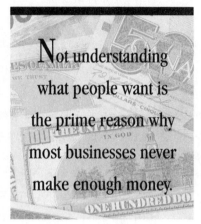

Not understanding what people want is the prime reason why most businesses never make enough money.

The invitation was then sent off with a free voucher for parking under the building.

When the prospect arrived, there was a host or hostess to meet them in the parking garage to escort them to the reception area. There was fresh juice or coffee waiting for them when they arrived. This change in strategy took the company from 60 percent occupancy to 92 percent within three weeks.

All this came from understanding and refocusing on the customer. Not understanding what people want is the prime reason why most businesses never make enough money. People will always be willing to pay you if you satisfy their needs and desires, or remove their frustrations, fears, or concerns.

If you get to know your customers—to understand them as intimately as I've described—you'll sense what it is they want. The closer you come and the more accurately you can predict what your potential customer really wants, the faster you'll get rich.

Sometimes what they want is obvious; sometimes it isn't. It is your ongoing responsibility to discover what it is they *do* want and to constantly adjust as you go along.

DON'T FOCUS ON MONEY AND YOU MAY JUST GET MORE OF IT

Vanessa Williams sang, "Sometimes the very thing you're looking for is the one thing you can't see." When it comes to money, these words ring true.

If you are in pursuit of money for money's sake—and that is your main focus no matter how hard you try—it will continue to elude you. Money is simply a currency for trading value or benefits. The sooner you take your focus off the money and bring a valuable product, service, result, or benefit to the market, the sooner you will start earning money.

The amount of money you earn will vary with the uniqueness of your product or service and the bigger your market or the market demand. But the central idea of focusing on giving value is true no matter what the product or what the market.

Someone said that you can't play tennis if you constantly have your eye on the scoreboard. It is the same deal with money. You can't focus on your customers and on delivering value if you're focusing on the money. And the more you focus on and pursue the money, the less will come your way, because your eye will not be on the game that counts.

Money is simply a by-product of delivering value to people. You cannot actually make money in business (unless you print it), you can only add value. It is this value that people want, and they will pay you for the privilege. So if you want to be rich, don't try to make money—just add value to people's lives.

GIVE YOUR CUSTOMERS ENOUGH REASONS TO WANT TO HAND OVER THE CASH

You've probably heard the old saying, "Build a better mouse trap and the world will beat a path to your door." Well, this is no longer true. There are companies all over the world building better and better mouse traps. All their products are available and competing with yours, and consumers aren't sitting around waiting for your product to hit the shelves. When you have a product, you need to take your offering to them and give them enough emotional and logical reasons to want it more than they want to keep their money or to buy somebody else's product or service.

Remember, people buy first through emotion. With the exception of professional buyers, most people don't make purchases based on logic. They make purchases because the product or service fulfills some emotional or psychological need. This is what people mean when they say "Sell the sizzle, not the steak." Usually, it is only after they buy that customers justify their purchase with logic.

This explains why customers often get "buyer's re-morse" shortly after making a purchase. If there's either too much hype or emotion used in making a sale, or too few log-ical reasons are given to customers to help them justify and feel comfortable with their decision, then buyer's remorse often sets in. Be sure to build enough emotion into a cus-tomer's buying decision, but don't leave them hanging with-out backing it up with logic. That way you avoid the regret that may set in after the sale is made.

Until recently, Alfa Romeo had this problem. People loved the image of their cars, their sportiness, and the feeling of Italian passion. But Alfa buyers often had regrets because Alfa's reliability and performance weren't good enough. Alfa couldn't supply enough reasons to support the emotional purchase. This can happen in virtually any scenario. How-ever, you have a greater danger of this occurring the more expensive a product or service is or the more uncertain the customer is about making that decision.

Alfa created unhappy customers by selling cars based on their status alone, making customers feel that the car gave them a good image. Cars also need to be practical and af-fordable, and they need to meet customer expectations. If not, customers will buy something else or cancel the sale. Alfa Romeo learned that the hard way.

In selling just about anything, you need to not only cre-ate great emotional feelings about buying your product or service, but also to have equally sound logical reasons to help customers justify their decision—or your sale will not proceed.

THE SECRET OF BECOMING A MARKETING GENIUS

What makes someone a marketing genius? How do they reach this status and what is it that they do? There is only one way—ask your customers what they want and then take it one step further. This is very easy to say, yet very hard to do without really understanding the point thoroughly.

You'll be happy to know that there is a single, powerful step you can take to find out exactly what your customers want. Go out and sit face to face with your customers. First target those people who have come in contact with your business yet didn't buy from you. Discover the reasons why they didn't buy, and then address them creatively. That's the secret; that's all it is. And that is where the gold is hidden.

Go out and sit face to face with your customers.

Doing it may not be easy for you. I find many people either don't want to hear complaints and bad news, or don't want to bother their customers. Even if they have something bad to say, the fact that you're there listening means they will view you and the company in a more positive way. Your customers, prospects, and those who have already refused you will all enjoy giving you some feedback. That feedback will tell you how to overcome their resistance and objections in the future.

They will see you as a company that cares. And if you ask the right questions, they'll give you all the information to develop winning marketing strategies. If you ask enough people, you'll see a trend develop. This will be all the information you need to build an exciting and profitable business.

The process is simple—politely ask them the questions outlined in the following and just sit back and listen carefully:

$ **Why did you choose not to purchase from us this time?**

$ **What could we do better next time?**

$ **What did you like about us, if anything?**

$ **What did you like about our competition that you feel we could adopt?**

I did some work like this for a well-known security company, whose sales at the time were very poor. By talking directly to customers, I discovered many ideas that have helped make that company worth tens of millions of dollars today. One idea was to put all their salespeople in uniform. Until then their sales team visited homes in dark suits. This intimidated their customers because people hate having door-to-door salespeople in their homes. When we made their salespeople look like security guards in uniform, customers felt more comfortable and secure. Within weeks this one discovery immediately increased sales by 30 percent.

Do not be tempted to have this research done by so-called expert research companies. It will be very expensive and will not give you the same value and insight that you'll get from doing it yourself—face to face with your customers. There are good research companies out there who know what they are doing and who will do a great job. But these people are hard to find, and you will still lose the power of doing it yourself. Having someone else do it risks wasting too much money and valuable insight. Trust yourself.

YOUR BUSINESS WILL GROW LIKE MAGIC!

This happens when a customer or employee realizes that you've done something wonderful for them—something far beyond their expectations. When you give them value in excess of what they felt they deserved or paid for, you have created a Magic Experience.

The aim of a Magic Experience is to make the transaction between you and your customers memorable. Magic Experiences leave a lasting positive impression, one that makes customers want to do business with you again. And Magic Experiences also make them happy to tell all their friends about the fun, exciting, and remarkable experience of doing business with you.

Magic Experiences leave a lasting positive impression, one that makes customers want to do business with you again.

To customers, a Magic Experience shows you care for them and what they do. To benefit from this, you must make Magic Experiences an integral part of your business—part of your systems—so they happen every time for every customer, so they appear to be a special event for each customer.

Each and every day, thousands of business transactions occur. You buy a paper, coffee, a bus ticket, gas for the car, a pair of shoes, lunch, an airline ticket, a coffee table, and so on. So many of these transactions are forgettable. Why? Because they are just the same as all the others.

Usually, the only buying experiences you remember are the bad ones—the surly waiter, the twelve phone transfers to find the right person, the dismissive "that's-just-how-it-is" answer. These sorts of experiences I call Murderous Experiences—because they murder your business. They're a thousand times worse than a forgettable one, because people never forget, they tell their friends, and they want revenge. On average, a person who is treated well in a transaction will tell two to five people. Treat someone badly, though, and they will tell an average of ten people! But provide a Magic Experience, and customers will become your most powerful, free, walking, talking advertisements.

All businesses can find a way to produce their own Magic Experience. How you do this depends on you and the type of business you're in. Brainstorm ideas with your staff, friends, and customers. Borrow ideas from other businesses that have impressed you. Be a little creative—a little different—because this is where the magic begins.

MAGIC EXPERIENCES TO REMEMBER

Remember, the more Magic Experiences you provide the more memorable your organization becomes and the more people will want to do business with you. Here are a few examples from several types of businesses for you to consider.

Health and Fitness Center

This center provides towels, baby-sitting, and fully stocked showers and dressing rooms, all free of charge. What's more, its staff bring patrons cold, purified water while they are working out. They stop for a chat, not about exercise but about life and things they have discovered interest you. When you leave, they offer to wash your work-out clothes and have them clean and ready for you on your next visit free of charge. Would you pay a little more to work out here?

A Car Dealership

When the sale is made, the salesperson casually asks about the customer's music preferences. When the car is delivered, not only is it shiny, new, and smelling beautiful, but there is $200 worth of your favorite type of music (CD or cassette) in the car as a gift—with a beautiful thank-you note. Will you recommend them to your friends?

A Restaurant

There's a restaurant that gives a free drink and snacks to all patrons who are waiting for a table. Staff regularly bring out samples of its entrees and desserts, offering them to those who are waiting. Not only does this keep people happy when waiting, but it encourages the sale of items patrons rarely order.

Men's Clothing Store

The minute you walk in you are offered a comfortable chair and a drink. Not just the usual tea or coffee—any drink you like: cola, cappuccino, freshly squeezed juice. You are greeted like a long-lost friend and never, ever asked "Can I help you?" If you simply got up and left after your drink and bought nothing, it would make no difference to their attitude. But I dare you to enter that shop and leave with nothing!

A Taxicab

Imagine getting into a cab and finding it comfortably air-conditioned, spotlessly clean, and well presented. A well-spoken driver offers you a piece of fruit or chocolate and a hand or face wipe. He also offers you a choice of newspaper or magazine and the use of a mobile phone if you need to call somebody. If you don't usually tip taxi drivers, you will this one.

Corner Store

Ever gone into a corner store hungry and arrived at the counter having eaten something while waiting in line? Imagine that when it's your turn to pay the cashier tells you that, because you were so hungry, the item you just ate is free. Would you return to this store?

HOW TO CREATE A LITTLE MAGIC IN YOUR BUSINESS

To create magic, you must be different—think outside the square. The rule is: Whatever others are doing, don't do that.

Start by saying thank-you to your customers in a meaningful way. Send them a note, a card, some flowers, or a gift basket. Call them later and tell them how much you appreciate their business. Give them the occasional freebie. Invite them back with a gift certificate.

Do small things that cost you very little but mean a lot to your customer. As someone once said: "The little things don't mean a lot—they mean everything!"

Do small things that cost you very little but mean a lot to your customer.

It pays off. I once referred a customer to a supplier. To say thank you, he sent me a gourmet hamper. It was quite expensive, I'm sure, but the sort of work he does is rarely under $8,000 to $10,000. The cost of a hamper looks pretty small next to that sort of money.

Push the boundaries of what you can offer and be meticulous on the detail. Near enough is not good enough anymore.

Introduce fun into your business and have fun with your customers. Go one step further. If everyone is offering their customers a cup of tea or coffee, offer them a cappuccino or a freshly squeezed orange juice. If everyone else starts doing cappuccinos and orange juices, offer a cocktail! It doesn't matter how; just be different.

CHAPTER 21

The Number-One Reason Why Most People Never Get Rich

The number one secret of commercial success is *be unique.* I cannot stress this strongly enough—you must offer solutions in products or services that no one else is offering. Most companies just go out there and do what everybody else is doing, especially from a customer's perspective.

This gets you nowhere. If you're not unique, you're like a tomato seller at the markets—you offer the same goods as everyone else, and all you can do to get more customers is drop your price. This is no way to get rich!

Ask yourself this question: Why are some things expensive and others cheap? It's because those that are expensive are unique, rare, or just hard to get. On the other hand, those that are cheap are usually easily obtainable.

If your aim is to make money, you should strive to make yourself unique, not just another commonly available commodity. When you produce something that's a commodity, there is nothing to differentiate you from anyone else, except price. That's exactly where you don't want to be, because inevitably you will have to drop your price and cut your margins to keep your customers. This will quickly make you broke.

Your goal in everything you do from now on, in setting up, running, maintaining, and developing your business, must be aimed at achieving this uniqueness.

Every aspect of your business—from developing or manufacturing your product or service to its promotion and delivery—must have a unique angle. And not only must it be unique, but its uniqueness must be understood and appreciated by a large enough group of customers (its market) to make its manufacture worthwhile.

It's a huge mistake to start, or run, a business thinking you're unique when you're not, or for some reason to keep your uniqueness a secret. In the 1980s IBM thought their PCs were unique—until they lost an entire market to clone PCs that did the same thing, but sold much cheaper. In the 1970s Xerox thought they were unique because they developed the commercial photocopier—until Canon started selling them at half the price.

WHY SHOULD I BUY FROM YOU RATHER THAN SOMEONE ELSE?

This is probably the most important question you can ask yourself! Astute marketers call the expression of uniqueness a "Unique Selling Proposition." I have heard it called many other things: a "Unique Buying Advantage," a "Value Proposition," and "Positioning." They all mean the same thing.

Personally, I prefer the term "Unique Selling Promise" (USP). A Unique Selling Promise is that special promise you make to your customer that only you can offer, which gives you an edge and compels your customer to want to buy from you rather than someone else.

Anthony Robbins—the charismatic self-development practitioner once said, "The quality of your life is in direct proportion to the quality of questions you ask yourself and others!" Heeding this good advice, you must continually ask yourself this question: Why should someone buy from me as opposed to my competition? In other words . . . Why should I buy from you?

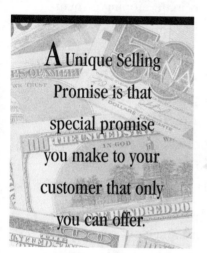

A Unique Selling Promise is that special promise you make to your customer that only you can offer.

When I ask my clients this question, I almost always get one of these two standard answers: "We offer better quality!" or "We offer better service!" I then ask them, "If I were to ask your competitor up the street the same question, what do you think they would say?" The answer is usually, "The same thing!" What this means from a customer's perspective—and especially a new customer who has never done business with you before—is that you are simply not unique. You are just the same as everyone else.

In other words, you are more of a commodity than you think. And if you are just a commodity in the eyes of a customer or prospect, you can't possibly charge as much as you would like or they will simply go somewhere else. Sometimes you cannot even charge enough to make a profit.

This means your only competitive advantage is your price and, as far as your customer is concerned, the lower your price the better. Customers don't know or care if you are making a profit, all they want is a competitive price, even if it is eating your heart out.

SO WHAT IS THE ANSWER?

If in reading the earlier sections you've discovered you aren't unique, there's only one thing to do—*make yourself unique.*

In order to do this you must now ask yourself: Why should someone buy from me as opposed to my competition?

This is *the* number-one secret to running a successful business. This is also the number-one reason why some people get very rich. They understand that uniqueness pays big dividends. How you do this is by developing a meaningful and powerful USP.

How you develop your USP is by discovering what it is that you can do or change to be unique. And you start doing this by *talking with your customers* or potential customers. They'll tell you—free of charge.

Your USP is the cornerstone of your marketing, and without it you cannot compete, nor will you ever get rich. If you do not have a USP, I suggest you stop everything and find one—now—today! Without a powerful USP, you have no positioning, no edge, no reason for customers to buy from you other than, perhaps, price. This is costing you a fortune in lost profits and lost sales.

Even if you find it hard at first to discover anything unique about what you do or produce, you must keep searching. If you want to get rich, you cannot do what everybody else does. You must be different, scarce, or unique. Becoming different, scarce, or unique is the reason why people will line up to buy what you have and pay top dollar to get it. So take a fresh look at yourself. How different, scarce, or unique are you?

THE QUICKEST WAY TO GET RICH

We've just discussed why most people never make money—because they don't have a USP. It makes sense, therefore, to say the quickest way to get rich is to create your own USP, no matter whether you're an individual or huge multinational. In many cases, the reality is that most people don't currently have one.

Sometimes a USP is obvious and quick to reveal itself. You may already be doing something unique and simply not letting your customers know about it. If this is the case, it's just a simple matter of starting to tell them what you're doing that will make you unique. At other times finding a USP can be a difficult, painful, and frustrating task. Eventually, finding a USP may require a whole change in strategy.

Your starting point, however, is always with your customers. Go out and ask them. Get to know what their fears, frustrations, desires, or concerns are with your company, your industry, or your product. Always do it face to face and do it yourself as much as possible.

Once you think you have found your USP, remember to test it first. Try it in a limited number of ads or brochures and compare the sales or query rates with your usual methods.

This is important, because you may be off the mark several times before you hit the jackpot. And remember, if someone else in your market is offering the same thing, your USP is therefore not unique and it is not a USP.

In developing your USP, you need to thoroughly understand the distinction that a USP is product- or service-specific. This means that a USP should usually apply to each product or service you offer.

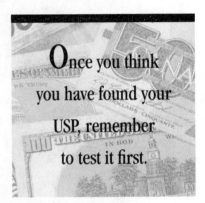

Once you think you have found your USP, remember to test it first.

Becoming unique gives you the massive advantage of offering your product or service in a way that nobody else does. If your customers want what you are offering—which they should if you've done the right research—you can almost always immediately raise your prices without fear, and this means an immediate rise in profits, too.

The best way to explain this is to give you some examples to which you can relate. The following examples of great USPs are mostly retail-focused, but USPs are equally applicable to any business, large or small, in any industry or market segment.

Plumbers Here's an advertisement (page 130) you might find in your yellow pages.

Does this business give you a compelling reason to seek out Joe's services? The obvious answer is no! Unfortunately,

The wrong way

as you can see, this gentleman has not developed a USP. Perhaps he actually does do something unique in delivering his service, but from his ad, he is certainly keeping it a secret from us. If Joe was to get to understand his customers—their real fears, frustrations, desires, and concerns—he would quickly realize that people who have dealt with plumbers, or tradesmen in general, are mostly concerned and frustrated about their punctuality. So the question is: Why is Joe's advertisement not addressing this frustration?

The right way

This advertisement is from a plumber who has been through the exercise of talking with his customers. He now offers his services on the basis that "If we're not there on time, your service call is on us." This is his USP. This is what makes him unique and helps him stand out from his competitors; he has made no secret of it by putting his unique offer in the headlines of his advertisements and on his shop window. You be the judge. If you needed a plumber today, which one would you call?

Obviously, most people would select the second plumbing business, because the ad gives us a compelling reason to do so. It makes a meaningful promise that appeals to our underlying frustrations and concerns. By reading this ad, we would want to test the promise it makes. If the ad lived up to our expectations and removed our frustrations and concerns, we would probably become happy long-term customers. If not, the business would be in a lot of trouble, doing a lot of free work, and eventually, inevitably, going broke quicker than it would have otherwise.

Now this is a very important point: If you can't live up to your USP, don't offer it! Another good point to make here is that the second plumbing business—before it had its USP—took pride in its plumbers being punctual. There were very happy clients already; just not enough. They simply didn't realize that this punctuality was something everybody wanted and that nobody else was offering it in the way they offer it now. Business has tripled in size since people's frustrations and concerns were addressed, and they were told about it with the USP!

Video stores What could be more of a commodity than a home video? Nearly every suburb has a video store or two. But how many of these stores have a USP?

Civic Video does, and it has been a huge success. They obviously did their homework. They found that customers were frustrated when they selected a movie and ended up not enjoying it. Most video stores adopt the "tough luck, try again" attitude, but Civic Video created a "love it or swap it free" USP. This instantly appealed to their customers, giving them a compelling reason to perhaps travel a little further to a Civic Video store and even to pay a little more.

In contrast VideoEzy, a competitor, could have just gone out and copied Civic Video, but they didn't, and neither should you with your competition. Their own research un-covered another strong customer need: They learned that customers also got frustrated when there were never enough copies of the lat-est-release blockbuster. Customers had to wait days, sometimes weeks, for a copy. So VideoEzy created their "get it first time or get it free" USP. Their customers obviously want to get exactly what they want when they want it, and are prepared to pay a bit extra for the service. Both Civic Video and VideoEzy have very good, but dis-tinctly different, USPs.

"Get it first time or get it free!"—VideoEzy

Federal Express   Most people are aware of the enor-mously successful USP used by FedEx, "Absolutely Positively Overnight," but what most people don't know is where FedEx began. Their USP used to be "We use our own planes." They thought this was meaningful and that it gave their customers a compelling reason to use their service. But business was obviously not good. FedEx was forced to take another look. What they discovered was that customers wanted a reliable overnight service. They didn't care how it got there or who owned the planes—so long as it got there when they wanted it there.

FedEx promptly changed their USP and offered their now world- famous "Absolutely Positively Overnight" promise. This simple change has helped FedEx become one of the biggest companies in the world.

"Absolutely Positively Overnight"

Domino's Pizza   "There in 30 minutes or it's free" is the USP that made Domino's Pizza famous. Their research discovered that the prime concern of people wanting home-delivered pizza was the time it took it to get there. So Domino's directly addressed that concern. Business took off instantly to make Domino's the biggest home-delivery pizza company in the world.

"There in 30 minutes or it's free"
—Domino's Pizza

Woolworths What do people want most when they buy their food? Woolworths, Australia's leading food retailer, found out it was freshness. They came up with their USP "Woolworths—The Fresh Food People." Now, let me ask you this: Do you think Woolworths' produce is any fresher than any other large supermarket's? Who knows. But I doubt it. Still, Woolworths grabbed this positioning to give them a distinct uniqueness. When you do this sort of thing, you get what Jay Abraham calls a "pre-emptive advantage," which means that you own that position in the market's perception because you came out and said it first. Even if your competitors come out after you to claim the same thing, they will be seen as simply copycats and will lose credibility.

No doubt Woolworths' food is fresh, but their promise makes it all the more believable!

Creating a USP can be a long process or a short one, and by its very nature it is not something you can copy. It needs to be unique to you. The best starting point is to find out from your (potential) customers why they would buy from you as opposed to anyone else. If you ask enough customers, you will find a pattern and great clues as to what you should be offering and how you should be offering it.

"The Fresh Food People"

WHEN IS A USP ABSOLUTELY CRITICAL?

The more competition you have (or the more of a commodity you are) the more important a USP becomes. If you discover a great USP, and shortly afterward your competitors begin to follow you and offer the same thing, then you need to get one step ahead again and offer your customers something new or some additional (added value) reason to buy from you again. If you offer something truly unique, and are the best at what you do, it will be difficult for your competitors to match you. So you need to keep improving your game, making it hard for your competition to follow. This is the key to a sustainable USP.

HOW TO RAISE YOUR PRICES AND PUT THOUSANDS OF EXTRA DOLLARS IN YOUR POCKET

As I said before, when you create a strong, compelling USP and deliver on it, you can almost always raise your prices. If you do this, some customers may leave you or choose not to do business with you any longer. That's all right—don't panic!

Some customers are just not profitable, and it's OK to let them go somewhere else. You can't afford to keep servicing them anyway if you can't make a profit on them.

If your USP is on the mark, I guarantee you will attract many new customers who will be happy to pay your price. In most cases, they'll pay without even hesitating. You can easily increase your price by at least 10 percent without any concern, and usually by more.

Let's consider: What will a 10, 20, or even 50 percent increase mean to your business? A lot. To many businesspeople's disbelief, this additional money goes straight to your bottom line and means a 10, 20, or 50 percent gross increase in your profits. This can add thousands of dollars to the value of your business.

Most customers are not price shoppers. Even the "cheapest price" customers are beginning to discover that the cheapest is not always best. What customers are really seeking is the best value. And value equals quality plus price.

It is your job, if you want to become rich, to educate your customers not about price but about what unique quality and service they will receive—before you even mention the price.

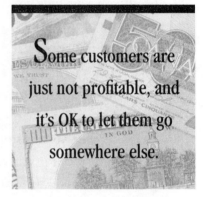

Some customers are just not profitable, and it's OK to let them go somewhere else.

This concept is even more important to understand if you're in a tight, competitive market. There are literally dozens of different ways to create a USP. If you discover you are not unique, or find it difficult to express a uniqueness in what you do, then adding value in a meaningful way is probably your answer to creating a uniqueness.

Adding value means giving or offering your customers something extra—something they are not accustomed to receiving from others; something that they don't expect. It may be a Magic Experience you've created, but it must represent value for your customers—so when they receive it, it makes them happy to pay the extra for it.

IT USUALLY COSTS YOU NOTHING— IT CAN MAKE YOU MILLIONS

If you are already doing something unique, but not telling your customers, making a few minor changes to your marketing to inform your customers of this uniqueness won't make any difference to your marketing budget but will make a massive difference to your customer response.

If you are running ads like the plumber's example we saw earlier in this section, all you need to do is change your headline to include your new USP. This undoubtedly will bring you more business with very little additional cost.

If you find, however, that you need to add value for your customers, or to create a USP, it may cost you some additional money. But remember you will be paying the same cost price as you always have for the added-value items or services, while your customers will perceive their value at the full retail price. It is this value-adding that helps differentiate you from your competitors, justifies paying your higher prices, and gives customers a feeling that you care about them.

Always follow this basic principle: Creating a USP will cost you very little extra. If done the right way, however, it can make you millions in extra profit and capital growth.

MAJOR CONFUSION—MISSION *vs* USP

There still remains much confusion between a mission statement and a USP. To help clear this up once and for all, a mission statement is essentially an internal communication; a USP is a directly external communication.

In other words, a mission statement is a statement outlining "what we do around here." This tells your entire team about your general goals and philosophies—how you go about your business. It can even define your terms of reference and help keep you on track about what new opportunities to chase and what to reject.

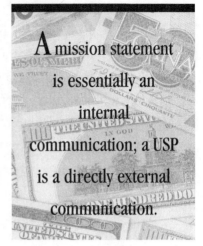

A mission statement is essentially an internal communication; a USP is a directly external communication.

A USP, on the other hand, is an external statement aimed at your customers. This statement is supposed to educate your customers very quickly about what you do and why they should buy from you.

Here is an example of the difference. These are the mission statement and USP we used at Vision.

VISION'S MISSION STATEMENT

At Vision, we don't just sell summaries and organize seminars—anybody can do that.

- We touch and impact many people's lives—both directly and indirectly.
- We help people in business foster the entrepreneurial spirit, make more money, employ more people, pay more taxes—which is good for our country.
- We help people achieve breakthroughs and grow personally and professionally.
- We empower people to help others grow. We are proud of what we do because we make a difference to people's lives.

One of Vision's USPs for the business book summary is, "Now you can read a business book in fifteen minutes." Keep in mind, too, that a mission statement and value statement (see page 75) are also different. Your value statement, while also an internal communication, gives your employees some strong guidelines about how they conduct *themselves* in their day-to-day approach to the business. The mission statement explains the business's aims.

The Death of Market Share

An astute marketer once said: "Business is no longer about market share but about the share of a single customer."

It may be a surprise to some people, but usually advertising or promotion isn't the best way to increase revenue. It is high risk and generally does not work as well as it should. Before you spend another cent and risk your business health on ineffective advertising, you first need to develop the cheap, low-risk alternatives for increasing your revenue.

THE CUSTOMER YOU HAVE IS WORTH THOUSANDS

Every business needs to implement the following three strategies to be successful:

Strategy 1—Constantly attract new customers.

Strategy 2—Develop ways to generate more revenue on each sale.

Strategy 3—Develop ways to ensure your customers purchase from you again and again.

If you are able to work vigorously on all three of these strategies, you are guaranteed to have a thriving, profitable business. The problem is that most businesses focus solely on the first strategy while largely ignoring the other two much cheaper and easier ways of generating revenue. When I first realized this, it made so much sense that I have been practicing and pushing it ever since. No business can thrive without addressing all these strategies simultaneously.

The following example demonstrates the power of this approach and its massive effect on profits.

This is massive growth in either case. A 10 percent increase in each element has produced not a 10 percent

---

GROWING FOR PROFIT

A business currently has $8,000,000 in annual turnover. The turnover is made up of 2,000 customers, an average transaction amount of $2,000, and an average two transactions per customer per year.

Compare what happens if all three elements are increased at first by just 10 percent, then by 25 percent.

Now
2,000 customers × $2,000 per average transaction
× 2 purchases per year per customer   **= $8,000,000**

If we were to work on each area of this business
simultaneously, and increase turnover by just 10%
in each area, the business would look like this:

10% Increase
2,200 customers × $2,200 per average transaction
× 2.2 purchases per year per customer   **= $10,648,000**

At 25% the business would look like this:

25% Increase
2,500 customers × $2,500 per average transaction
× 2.5 purchases per year   **= $15,625,000**

growth in the business, but a 33 percent growth. If we had not realized this, and just focused on attracting new customers (Strategy 1), there would have been an increase of only 10 percent.

A 25 percent growth in each area leads to a massive 95 percent growth overall. This 95 percent sounds remarkable, yet for any business it is easily achievable with this three-pronged approach—but growing new customers alone will never do it.

New Customers Simply Cost More

When a business starts, it has no option but to focus on getting new customers. But once this has been achieved, the other two strategies must be used to make the business a real success.

Allocating all your resources toward attracting new customers is the most expensive and least profitable strategy for business development. It costs you about six times more (on average) to attract a new customer than it does to do business with an existing customer. The impact of this on your ability to generate revenue and profits is huge. When you begin to use the combined strategy we just discussed, and maximize your existing customers, things rapidly change for the better.

Remember, a customer who has done business with you is likely to be happy with you and feel comfortable with you. This means that your most recent customers are your best prospects for buying something else from you for an immediate new transaction, a cross-sale, or an add-on sale. If you waste that chance, you kill your own success.

It costs you about six times more (on average) to attract a new customer than it does to do business with an existing customer.

BUILDING YOUR BUSINESS CAN BE REALLY CHEAP AND EASY

What can you do to implement the three strategies? If you are prepared to look, there are more effective, lower-risk, and lower-cost opportunities for improving your sales and profitability than just increasing your advertising.

Six ideas that beat increasing advertising every time include:

$ Adding value, or creating a new USP

$ Increasing your prices

$ Increasing loyalty and repeat business

$ Cross-selling or selling other products in your range

$ Up-selling or increasing the value of what is sold

$ Converting more prospects into paying customers

If you focus on these six overlooked opportunities in your business before you even think about advertising, you will find it produces low-risk profits you've never had before. I'm not suggesting that you should never increase your advertising; but you should do this only after you have maximized all these other opportunities in your business. Once you are maximizing your sales at this low risk, then you can take your profits and reinvest them into advertising.

These six ideas fall under the three strategies we looked at previously.

BUILDING YOUR BUSINESS

Attract new customers	Add value or build to a new USP
	Convert more prospects
Generate more revenue on each sale	Increase your prices
	Up-sell each customer
	Cross-sell
Make your customers buy again	Increase loyalty and repeat business

I discussed adding value and increasing prices when I talked about developing your USP. The key things to look at now are increasing customer loyalty, cross-selling, and up-selling.

YOUR BUSINESS MAY BE A LEAKING BUCKET

In big-picture terms it's very simple: To have a successful business, you must attract and hold onto customers faster than you lose them.

All businesses lose customers. But the more successful you want to be, the more you need to hold onto your customers. And the longer you can hold onto them, and the more you can make them want to buy from you, the more successful you'll be.

If you are constantly attracting new customers but not keeping them, you're suffering from what I call the "leaking bucket" syndrome, illustrated on page 146.

To become truly successful, you need to plug those holes in your business before you do anything else. You'll waste a tremendous amount of money and time if you try to increase

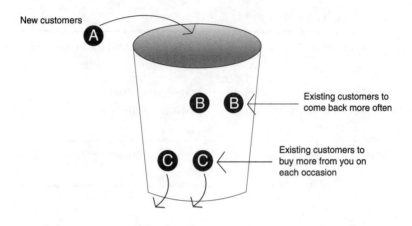

New customers

Existing customers to come back more often

Existing customers to buy more from you on each occasion

A without addressing Band C. If you dedicate yourself to B and C, you will see immediate improvements in both sales and profits.

How you dedicate yourself to B and C involves all the things I talk about in this book. You must get to know your customer, provide a Magic Experience, test your USPs, take the risk from your customer, and build a staff culture and attitude that makes the difference.

"WOULD YOU LIKE SOME FRIES WITH THAT?"

Customers purchase things because they have a need they want to satisfy. Usually, however, people buy more than one thing at a time or they buy again soon after a purchase. How many times have you gone out to buy something and come back with it and a lot more?

This happens frequently because satisfying one need often brings another to the surface. Customers usually buy in a sequence of products or services. If you recognize this, you can cash in on it.

Cross-Selling

When you get to know your customers intimately, you'll soon be able to identify sequences in their buying behavior. You can use this knowledge to build a range of secondary products and services that your customers will want. This is called cross-selling. You see the best companies and businesses doing it all the time. In fact, they've systematized it. Take McDonald's: "Would you like fries with that?" is a classic cross-sell. And why do they do it? Because they know that one in three people will say yes, and that one little question asked thousands of times a day is worth millions of dollars they would otherwise not get.

The Front and Back Ends

To have a great business, you need to have a good front end and back end. All businesses have front- and back-end opportunities.

The front end involves the first purchase a customer makes. The back end involves selling other products that are related, or part of a sequence that the customer may want. For example, a customer may buy a hammer. In this case the front end is the hammer, and the back end? It may be some nails. If, on the other hand, someone came in and bought some nails, then the nails would be the front end and the hammer the back end. But the back end wouldn't just stop with the hammer. There would be a whole range of things to sell: nail punches, nail removers, putty, wood glue, plaster, and so on.

The front end of your business involves new customers and purchases, and relates to Strategy 1—getting new customers. The back end of your business relates to Strategies 2 and 3—making the most of customers you have.

You can develop a very profitable business based on attracting customers for one purchase, and then offering a string of other profitable purchases. Even seemingly one-time purchases can easily turn into repeat purchases like haircuts, where customers may come back for years.

The problem is that most people in business only focus on the front end and forget about the back end—this tends to be ignored or happen by accident. You need to always have a conscious strategy to work your front and back ends simultaneously so as to maximize your sales and profits. If you have many products and services to sell on the back end, especially high-priced and profitable products, you can afford to spend more to attract new customers than if you have only a one-time, no-repeat sale. You can do this because you'll make up the profit by up-selling and cross-selling once you have them as a customer. I will cover this profit-generating idea more fully in a chapter on advertising expenditure. These two ideas link together.

It's far easier, far cheaper, and far more profitable to develop new products or services to sell to your existing customers than to develop new markets by trying to sell one product to the world.

When Customers Ask for a Tap, Sell Them the Sink

One of the best ways of increasing your profits is to seek to increase the value of what you sell. This is commonly known as an up-sell. You do this when you know you have the opportunity of offering a customer a slightly different product from what they first thought they needed, when that different product meets their needs more exactly and is more profitable for you.

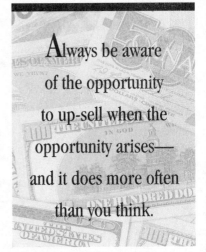

For example, say you sell sofas. A customer comes in with a budget of $1,000. When you identify her need by asking the right questions about use, positioning, and decor, you may think a slightly more expensive, $1,200 model will suit her better, because it will last longer and seat more people. On the basis that the $1,200 lounge meets your customer's needs best, you can and should quite easily be able to ethically sell her the more expensive and profitable product.

The important rider is that you don't try to push something that the customer doesn't want. We've all experienced a salesperson pushing the product that makes him more commission—and it isn't pleasant.

The key point here again is: You have to be sure you understand your customers' needs and that you are genuinely giving them something they want.

Always be aware of the opportunity to up-sell when the opportunity arises—and it does more often than you think. Most businesses just miss out on this simple opportunity to increase revenue and profits.

CHAPTER 23

Make It Easy for Customers to Buy

Many companies are still making it hard for customers to buy—whether it's bad customer service or customer unfriendly practices and policies. This isn't bad for business; it's criminal, and it may be killing your business.

Make yourself a customer for a day, and call or drop in as if you were a customer. How was the phone answered? How were you greeted? What barriers did you experience physically and emotionally? Would you want to do business with your company again?

How Taking the Risk Will Double or Triple Your Sales

In the old days, customers used to have to accept the risk of buying something from you. The unwritten rule was *caveat emptor*—Let the buyer beware! The buyer had to accept the risk that the product might not work, or suit their needs, or do what it claimed to do.

Many businesspeople still haven't realized that those days are long gone. Business thinking is now the exact opposite. Today the unwritten rule is: Let the seller beware!

The single greatest reason people don't buy (it is thought to be a staggering 80 percent of all the reasons) is that they perceive some level of risk in doing business with you. Therefore it stands to good reason that if you, as the seller, are able to do something to remove this risk—real or perceived—you will then have an automatic 80 percent better chance of completing every business transaction.

You can do this by offering your customers the opportunity to do business with you on a completely risk-free or low-risk basis.

Here are some simple ways to help remove your customers' perceived risk:

$ Let them sample or trial your product free of charge
$ Let them purchase at a low introductory price
$ Offer them a full, unconditional money-back guarantee (or, if you must, a conditional money-back guarantee)
$ Offer to pay a penalty if you don't perform, such as 110 percent of your money back if you're not totally satisfied

Today you have to seriously consider having this as an important part of your marketing strategy. The old days of *caveat emptor* are well and truly behind us. There is too much competition out there and too few customers. Also, today's customers are smarter, better educated, much more forceful and confident, and have myriad avenues for their complaints.

You must also be prepared to put total faith in the products or services you offer and stand behind them with an honest guarantee. If you can't guarantee your products or services, not only are you missing out on a great marketing opportunity, but your product is clearly something that you shouldn't be selling.

Any fear you have that people will take unfair advantage of you is unfounded. The good news, which has been proven over and over again, is that 99 percent of people are honest and will not take advantage of you. The few who may try it will be far outweighed by the increased business you will enjoy.

In many cases, simply taking the risk away from your customer will make you unique in your industry. And if you can't find a USP, this risk-reversal strategy alone may give you the uniqueness you need. Think about it! It's really common sense. It's so much easier to sell something when you can tell people: "If you don't like it, just return it and we'll give you a full, no-questions-asked refund."

Of course this exact offer is not feasible or possible in all situations, but in every situation you can take a step closer than your competition to removing the risk away or reducing it, creating more confidence in the buyer to try you out.

Addressing people's perceived risk with a separate guarantee, or as your USP, is not just a gimmick as some would believe. It's an honest way to make a genuine offer, while at the same time negating the major concern of all customers—risk.

Remember to Ask Your Customers

If you're having trouble working out what your risk-removal offer should be, just do exactly the same thing as you did to find your USP—ask your customers. Sit down and get to know their needs, desires, and concerns. The best advice I can give is that your existing and prospective customers will give you all the ideas you need.

SIMPLE BARRIERS FOR BUYERS WILL BREAK YOU

Making it easy to buy isn't just about risk reversal; it's also about making every step in the buying process as simple and friendly as possible.

Take a company whose customers order by mail. Is the form as simple as it could be? Are the instructions clear? Do they ask for any information they don't need? Is a stamped, addressed envelope included? All these things make it easier for people to buy. A range of payment options might help. And there is no excuse for not accepting credit cards.

Watch how people buy from you, analyze each step, and see how you can make it easier.

What about a retail business? Is the parking good (or as good as it can be)? Is the entry clear and inviting? Do you have customer-friendly signs to indicate what products are where? Do you provide baskets, carts, or even staff to carry the goods? Have you worked out where the best place is for bags, boxes, carts, and displays?

Watch how people buy from you, analyze each step, and see how you can make it easier. Usually you can make simple changes that won't cost you much but they'll add enormously to your bottom line.

You Can't Sell Dog Food to Dogs

I have often made this mistake myself, and I've seen many other people waste valuable time and money doing it. It is especially common if you're selling to big organizations with many divisions.

I'm talking about trying to sell to someone who can't buy from you. You must make sure the person you're talking to is in a position to make a buying decision. If you're speaking to the wrong person, it doesn't matter how good your product or your pitch is, you won't sell a thing.

The most effective use of your energy is discovering the power brokers in the organization (or family, when selling to individuals), and to identify exactly who you should be selling to.

Don't be deceived into thinking that a director or CEO is the right person. Often they aren't. Frequently the buying decision is made by a lower-level manager, a divisional director or, in smaller companies, the director's secretary. Many CEOs, directors, and managers are simply figureheads who smooth the waters and keep the status quo. These are the last people to sell to. They are risk-averse, will want to research everything, and can take months to decide.

I have seen people spend more on research than they would in simply buying from you. This is because they can justify research to help them make the "right" decisions, but an outright gut-feeling purchase feels too risky and will not be made.

The key here is: Don't get frustrated and give up. Simply do your homework, spend your time and creative energy trying to get in front of the right person, and, when you do, come out with all guns blazing as you may get only one opportunity.

This principle is especially applicable when it comes to marketing or advertising. Many people place ads that are either poorly targeted or poorly written. If an ad doesn't adequately address reader needs by offering a USP in the headline, you're trying to sell to people who can't, or won't, buy.

Advertising Can Kill Your Business

A dvertising your products or services isn't always a good idea. And by advertising I mean any form of communication, including selling, sales promotions, public relations, publicity, direct mail, and so on. You don't have to do any of it to increase your business.

You may be wasting most of your money. It still amazes me that advertising is one of the few areas where people seem content to keep paying money without getting anything in return. Ineffective advertising and promotions do little but drain valuable cash resources for little return. And ineffective advertising is the single largest cause of losses and failures in business.

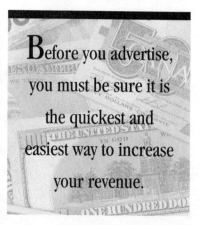

Before you advertise, you must be sure it is the quickest and easiest way to increase your revenue.

You must always view spending money on advertising or promotions in the same way as you would putting your money into any financial investment. Before you advertise, you must be sure it is the quickest and easiest way to increase your revenue. Explore other marketing options first. If advertising is something you feel you need to do, ask yourself the same sorts of questions you'd ask with other financial investments, no matter how small the amount:

$ How secure is it?
$ When do I get the money back that I invest?
$ What is the return on investment?
$ What is the guarantee?
$ Am I testing all my advertisements and measuring the results effectively?
$ Is my advertising using the most effective USP?
$ Am I getting the best prices and media positions for the placement of my advertisements?

Please use your common sense when it comes to the writing, buying, and placing of advertisements. Ask yourself—if you saw your own ad, would it make you want to go out and buy your product?

You must take into account the chances of seeing your ad as well. This is a very important point. If you have to look too hard to find your ad, or watch too long to see it, or listen too hard to hear it, your potential customers will have even more trouble because they won't be looking for it! It must jump out and grab their attention.

ONE OUT OF 1,400—YOU HAVE BETTER ODDS AT THE RACES

I have heard advertising guru Simon Reynolds claim we are exposed to more than 1,400 advertising messages per day.

With that amount of competition, it's very hard to get your customer's attention, no matter who you are. So hard that on average people remember just one of those 1,400 messages. This is a dismal success rate. Yet businesses still persist with these ineffective advertising practices. It's insane.

The whole area of advertising and promotions is a minefield. Every day businesses get seduced and blow their money—money that could be used much more profitably applying many of the other concepts we are discussing in this book. Consider the consequences of the two advertisements. Each cost $5,000 to place. One works, one does not. Notice what a huge financial difference each makes to the value of the business:

AD IT UP

	Ad A	*Ad B*
New Sales from Ad	$25,000	$3,000
Cost of Goods Sold	$12,500	$1,500
Gross Profit	$12,500	$1,500
Less Cost of Ad	$5,000	$5,000
Profit	$7,500	-$3,500
Return on investment	150%	-70%

The difference between the return on investment for the two ads is 220 percent.

If we start with Ad A, the one that works, let's see what effect it has on the business. The $5,000 spent on the advertisement produced $25,000 in sales, leaving a gross profit of $7,500 without any overhead allocation. The return on investment (ROI) for this ad is 1.5, or 150 percent. This is pretty good, especially if this happens over a month or so.

Looking at the second advertisement, Ad B, we see the cost is still $5,000, but it produces only $3,000 in sales. This leaves an incremental loss of $3,500. This is shocking! With Ad B the difference in lost sales is $22,000. This doesn't even take into account the loss from the repeat sales those new customers would bring in the future.

If this is not recognized and stopped immediately, it will ruin the business. In many cases businesses don't even track the origin of their sales, so they can't recognize the problem. Businesses can't afford to waste money on advertising that doesn't generate a healthy ROI.

There is, however, one exception to this rule—the only time it makes sense to lose money on advertising is when you have a big and very profitable repeat sales opportunity. This then justifies using loss-leader advertising as a means of acquiring customers you'll make a profit from later on. Advertising and promotions serve only one purpose: to make an immediate sale or bring you a new customer.

BRAND BUILDING ALONE IS A COP-OUT

There's a lot of talk about advertising and promotions building brand awareness or goodwill. In my view, this is a cop-out.

Advertising is just another way of selling your product, and if it doesn't sell, it isn't working. Money spent on advertising must be used to directly produce sales or new customers and can still build brand awareness effectively at the same time. These two functions should not be separated.

A great definition of advertising is that it is simply "salesmanship in print." How else can you justify it otherwise? It would be absurd to send your salespeople out to increase brand awareness or build goodwill, then tell them that it's all right not to make a sale. If that's obviously absurd, why accept similar claims for your advertisements, which is just selling in print?

Advertising and promotions is a dangerous game for the naive or unskilled. You must make sure your strategy is right before you commit and, if you do, test it slowly and carefully to be sure you are getting results first before you expand.

HOW MUCH SHOULD YOU SPEND ON ADVERTISING?

This is one of the most frequently asked questions in marketing, yet one rarely answered adequately. If you know exactly the right amount to spend, it will save you and make you millions!

Without a clear answer, businesses have resorted to allocating 5, 7, or 10 percent of turnover to advertising. This is totally the wrong approach, as you may be spending too little or too much. The right way to achieve the correct advertising budget is by using a method of Jay Abraham's called Marginal Net Worth (MNW), which refers to the lifetime value of the customer. The MNW calculation tells you what average profit a new customer will generate over the customer's lifetime.

MNW is the expected gross margin you will get from a new customer, less the cost of attracting that new customer.

To work it out for yourself, you need to know the expected gross margin of a new customer and the average advertising or marketing cost of finding that new customer.

The Expected Gross Margin

This is the amount of profit before overhead a new customer will generate for you over his or her time with your business. This will depend heavily on your ability to satisfy them and keep them buying from you. We looked at this in previous sections on Strategies 2 and 3 (see page 141).

Every business and every customer is different, so lifetimes will be different in each case. If your business is new or you have not been tracking this information, you have to predict this as best you can—making conservative estimates.

For example, if supermarket customers on average shop every ten days, that's thirty-six times per year. If the average amount spent is $100, and a customer on average lives in the area and shops at the store for five years, then the expected revenue every new customer brings is $3,600 per year over five years ($36 \times 100 \times 5$). This adds up to $18,000 in sales. For this example the gross margin is 25 percent, or $4,500.

EXPECTED GROSS MARGIN

Shops/year	36
Average spending	$100
Average revenue/year	$3,600
Average cost of goods/year	$2,700
Average gross profit/year	$900
Average gross profit/5 years	$4,500

This gives you a much better idea of how much to spend to attract a new customer. Using this method you can see that a customer is not worth $100, but up to $4,500.

If you saw your customer value as only $100 per customer, and you used 5 percent of turnover on advertising, you would spend only $5 to attract a new customer. If, however, you knew your MNW was $4,500, you could spend up to $4,499 per customer on advertising and still come out ahead.

Average Advertising Cost of a New Customer

You need to test your advertising and measure how many customers you get from each advertisement. This will clarify what it costs you to attract each new customer. Let's assume that you place an ad for $15,000, and you get 100 new customers from this ad. The average cost of a new supermarket customer is $150. This is more than their average amount spent on the first purchase, but it is still acceptable to keep running those ads. Why? Because you are going to get another $4,350 from that customer over the next five years.

Once you've worked all this out, your goal is to keep this $150 cost in mind, and then develop more cost-effective advertising to acquire new customers. In the process, you must constantly test media, offers, copy, and strategy to reduce this cost.

The very astute businessperson will also realize that the lifetime value of a customer is not fixed. Nor are the gross margin and customer acquisition cost. It is your job to find ways of bringing the acquisition cost down and the margin up.

This is what I talked about earlier in this section. The quickest and most profitable way to grow your business and get rich is to increase the average transaction value (increasing the price or unit of sale, and so on) and increase the transaction frequency (repeat sales and complementary sales) for each customer. You can grow your business by constantly looking, not only to increase the number of new customers with advertising and better sales conversion ratios, but also to increase the unit of sales and repeat business.

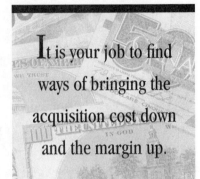

It is your job to find ways of bringing the acquisition cost down and the margin up.

If you do all three of these together, your business will grow exponentially, as will the lifetime value of your customers, as will your advertising budget, and so on.

So do not just take an arbitrary 5, 7, or 10 percent of sales, as this may be totally wrong for you. The key here is to understand what a new customer is really worth to you, now and in the future. Then use that information to ensure you have an adequate advertising budget to effectively grow your business.

How to Get Someone Else to Pay for Your Advertising

We've already seen how advertising is the last option you should use to build your business, because it is the most expensive and the least effective.

There are other ways to advertise your business that are free, or where you have to pay only when you are guaranteed a sale. This is a far cry from paying for an ad, whether it brings you a new customer or not.

How you do this is quite simple. First you must realize that people (your customers) do not make purchases in isolation. Customers usually buy in patterns, in groups of products, or in a sequence. Sometimes customers do not even realize this themselves. One purchase triggers another, and another, and another, and most customers do not even know about the next product or service in the sequence. It's only when they make a purchase that they realize they need the next one.

Here's a simple example. If you want to buy a car, what you really want is a car that will get you from A to B. But

Customers usually buy in patterns, in groups of products, or in a sequence.

once you've bought the car, you suddenly realize you need insurance. Now did you want insurance? No, you wanted a car; and now that you have a car, you need air-conditioning in the car, maybe some more CDs or cassettes to listen to while you drive, maybe some seat covers, or some soap, polish, or a hose to wash the car. Now tell me, when you thought about buying a car, did you think about *all* those other purchases? Most likely not.

If you have been selling cars for a while, you may begin to see a pattern—that most people will require all, or some, of these products. If you are a seller of car wash facilities, and recognize this, you can approach the person who is selling cars to direct their customers to you by giving every person who buys a new car their first three washes free. How do you do this? You simply give the salesperson three complimentary vouchers to give to their clients when they deliver a new car. The car seller should be happy to do this, because it doesn't cost them anything, it makes them look good to the customer, it shows they care, and it adds value for the customer.

The customer will most likely want to keep their new car clean and will happily come to you because you have been recommended by the person they've just bought from.

Now you may have to do the three washes for nothing, but chances are if you're good at making that car shine, and have an attractive weekly washing rate, you will be able to sell that customer a car wash package for six, twelve, or more car washes.

What has it cost you to get this new customer? Three free washes! This is better than running ads that don't work and standing around waiting for a customer to call!

This methodology can be used with just about every business. If you're not doing it (or not doing it correctly), it is costing you a fortune in lost sales and wasted advertising dollars.

Think about your own business and your customers. Simply ask yourself: Where do your potential customers go before they come to you? Where do they go while they're buying from you? Where do they go after they have bought from you? By doing this you've identified the businesses that have your customers.

Start approaching these other businesses and establishing relationships with them. Make sure you make them attractive offers—such as an extra service for their customers. They won't do it just because you ask, so you need to give them a great benefit for their clients. These could be vouchers, demonstrations, discounts—whatever works best for your product and your industry.

This is a powerful new business generator. Not only do you get free advertising, but you also get a strong endorsement from someone who has credibility with their customers.

How to Double Your Business Turnover Without Spending Another Cent

Most business owners still believe that to double your business you need to double the number of new customers, or at least double your inquiry rate. The good news is that this is simply untrue!

Let me give you a simple example to show you what I mean. One of our clients builds display homes. He came to us because his advertisements were not pulling the way they used to, and business was dropping off. Most people in this situation want me to create a brilliant new advertisement that will have customers clamoring at the door. In these circumstances creating an advertisement is probably the last thing you should be doing.

We asked this builder how many customers were responding to the current advertisements before business dropped off. He replied that they got about 250 inquiries every two weeks. Now he was getting only about 200.

What this meant in real terms was that his advertising was 20 percent less effective than before. In addition, we discovered another statistic that was more important—he was making only three sales from the 200 inquiries he was getting every two weeks. Just three sales, and he was happy with it. That's a conversion rate of just 1.5 percent.

The main problem wasn't the 20 percent loss in advertising effectiveness, but the low sales conversion of 1.5 percent. Our goal was not to fix his advertisements, but to get him some sales training and double his turnover. If we could fix his selling process, and get his conversions up to six or even nine sales out of 200—not a huge conversion rate—he would double or triple his business despite the 20 percent fall in inquiries.

Most managers don't see it this way, but a lost or wasted lead is just as bad as, or even worse than, lost stock in manufacturing. In the case of the builder, losing 98.5 percent of his potential customers should be viewed in exactly the same way as losing 98.5 percent of raw materials in the manufacturing process. No company could afford that, nor would anyone put up with it—except, it seems, in marketing.

50 Percent of Something Is Better Than 100 Percent of Nothing

When you look around at others who have made money, usually you can only see the idea, product, or service. Quite often it is pretty simple—something so obvious that you feel you have a hundred ideas that would be better products.

But nine times out of ten, people who make lots of money don't have the best idea, product, or service. What they have is the best application of an idea. What counts is what you do with the idea and how you put it to commercial use.

How you put it to commercial use will depend on many things, such as your resources: what contacts, influence, mental strength, capital, reputation, power, marketing, and

advertising skills you have. If that sounds like a lot for someone starting out in business, it is.

That's why rich and powerful people always seem to get
richer and more powerful. They know how to apply any
ideas they have. They have the capital resources and the reputation to motivate people to make these ideas a success.
They understand marketing and they have the right people
around them. All this ensures mistakes are minimized and
opportunities are maximized. Because of this, backing or endorsement from the right person can make or break your
product idea. When you're starting a business, look for opportunities to get involved with such people or organizations. You may think this is difficult. I can assure you from
my experience that it is a lot easier than trying to do it all
yourself. When I started Vision Publishing, I did it in partnership with one of the leading businesses in Australia. I
gave up a large portion of equity in the business, and in return I got access to all those resources I didn't have. Without
that deal Vision wouldn't have gotten up and running, and I
wouldn't have had the chance to learn what I did.

Finding a partner or investor may take time and cost you
some equity in the idea, but remember, 50 percent of something is always better than 100 percent of nothing.

HOW TO GET INVESTORS TO
HUNT YOU DOWN

People or organizations with lots of resources rely on new
ideas and good people to keep them growing. Because of this
basic need in the market, if you have faith in your idea and

confidence in yourself, it will be easier than you think to sell your concept to investors.

However, calling and asking for an appointment with a possible investor is simply not good enough. Everyone else does it, the chances of it happening are very slim, and its sloppiness impresses nobody. You must prepare yourself fully beforehand with a comprehensive and exciting business plan—one that's well researched and put together. You need all the facts and figures and all the answers ready. This all has to be packaged in a professional presentation. No doubt you've heard this before, and with good reason—it's common sense.

Treat your search for investors as you would a world-class product launch.

Treat your search for investors as you would a world-class product launch. You might advertise for a joint venture partner or venture capitalist in the magazines or newspapers they read. You might contact targeted companies directly with a creative direct mail piece, followed by a phone call. You might seek some publicity for your idea and see what interest that generates. Or you may have to launch your product or service first in a small way and get the idea into the market, then give it the credibility that will attract interested parties.

None of this will work, however, if you are missing two vital ingredients—passion and enthusiasm. If you are not genuinely excited and passionate about your ideas, how can you expect anyone else to throw money at them? You can't get a brilliant business partner or investor if you aren't enthusiastic about your potential success.

Having enthusiasm doesn't mean you need to jump up and down when presenting your idea, but when you are excited from within it will show through. There is no quicker way to blow a presentation and turn an investor off than to come across as being unexcited about your idea. Your passion is your greatest selling tool.

If you want investors to hunt you down, you must be well prepared, be different, and, above all else, be passionate about your business idea.

CHAPTER

What's the Magic Button for Business Success?

In this section I've covered many ways to develop your business through marketing. Of all these techniques, which one should you use? All of them! But don't try to do everything at once. Apply common sense to these good marketing principles as you would to anything else.

Look at the entire sales and marketing process first and find the weakest link. Then work on improving that first. Always search for the result that will provide the biggest and most dramatic increase in business. Work it through, and then be smart in how you implement it.

PART FOUR

Your People

CHAPTER

How to Get Your
Employees to Fall
in Love with
Your Company

I've emphasized that your people are your greatest asset and one of the four critical ways you can gain a competitive advantage. So how does this work?

If your people are positive and happy to be working for you, you're way ahead. No one, I repeat no one, can compete with individuals who enjoy their work, who have fun with customers, and who actually care about customers. Your competitors can't copy such a brilliant culture overnight. Your people, and the culture around those people, are the heart and soul of your business. This means that getting, keeping, and leading good people is one of the most valuable things you can do. It's important to know how to develop this competitive advantage and how to get the most from your people.

I've observed a lot of company cultures, and the way they treat and reward their people always amazes me. It's a wonder they manage to keep any staff at all—and it shows in their performance and the company's bottom line.

Most businesses seem to forget that all employees are people—they have hopes, fears, desires, and problems like everyone else. They don't leave their emotions at home when they go to work. And as much as is possible, you should always try to treat them all equally and with respect no matter what job they do. Your employees, from the cleaners to the top executives, all need nurturing and tender care to bring out the best in them.

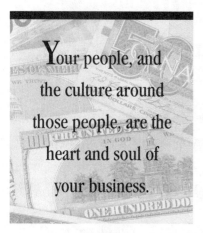

Your people, and the culture around those people, are the heart and soul of your business.

My father once told me that you should treat important people as if they were unimportant, and unimportant people as if they were important. This is a pretty useful piece of advice whenever you meet someone who is not on your own social and economic level. *Respect is* the key word. There is never any reason to show disrespect to your employees, no matter who you are.

Even though someone may not know as much as you, have as much money as you, be as old as you, or have as strong a personality as you, respect for the individual is a must. And it almost goes without saying that gender, ethnicity, and religion are not a basis for treating anyone as different. It's as much a question of your personal foundations as it is of managing your people.

In fact, the more authority and power you have, the more you need to respect others' feelings and situations. It's part of being a great leader. Consistency is the key. It's no good to be respectful only when you're feeling good.

The Best Businesses Have the Best Leaders

The best businesses have great leaders, and great leaders know it's their power that constantly supports and lifts others around them. Great leaders inspire others to become more, especially when times are tough. It's in these times that leadership shows—as a leader you may feel you have more reason than anyone else to be stressed and on a short fuse. It is especially important at times like these that you show courage, share your power, and inspire your people to push through. And remember to share a laugh and make it clear that, no matter what happens, you'll be steady and in charge. That's what great leadership is.

I was on the receiving end of a great piece of leadership from my partner on one occasion. It is something that will stay with me forever as a great example.

We were on the eve of our first major seminar, one I had organized and arranged with Jay Abraham in just nine days to coincide with the launch of his new publication. We had never been in the seminar business before; anyone in this industry could have told us that doing this in nine days was insane. Most seminars for around 900 people take at least three months to organize. Yet our naiveté allowed us to think this was achievable in nine days.

We mailed invitations to our customer base to attend the seminar. We arranged a venue, and ticket sales were coming in thick and fast. We filled 900 seats in four days flat, yet money just kept pouring in. With two days to go, we had received payment for 1,200 seats, with no way to stop the flow or to inform our customers that we had sold out. We improvised by squeezing additional seating into the theater to accommodate this unstoppable flow of sales. Our phones were ringing hot with customers wanting additional seats for friends they wanted to bring along. When they were told we were sold out, they didn't believe it as the tickets had only just gone on sale. They started to get irritated and called me directly to insist I get them in.

In the meantime I had arranged on short notice to get a celebrity master of ceremonies—one famous for selling product on TV. At midnight on the night before the seminar, with total chaos around me and extreme pressure on both me and my people to try to deal with this new adventure, our MC friend decided he wanted to renegotiate his fee up by $5,000 or he wasn't showing up.

This was a real blow and left me standing cold trying to think who I could get of that caliber with just eight hours to go. I wasn't used to doing business that way, and I was angry to say the least. We didn't have the budget to pay this additional money, and besides I didn't want him anyway if that's how the man did business. After exhaustively trying to get a replacement, I called my partner to inform him that we didn't have an MC and that we were just going to have to do without one. He knew how hard we had been working to pull this off and sensed my anger and frustration.

Without even batting an eye he said: "Don't worry, I'll fix it; I'll make sure the MC is there in the morning. You go get some sleep."

I later discovered my partner had called this gentleman and paid his increased fee from his own pocket. At first glance that seemed like quite an easy fix, but why this course of action deserves to be applauded stems from the simple fact that very few people will look to a solution that involves personal financial loss. It was a tough decision taken quickly, which enabled the overall success of the project. In the scheme of things, the additional money was not that much, but without my partner's leadership and calmness in that situation, we would have ended up without an MC. And I would have been up all night trying to make other plans.

The end result was that we had 1,500 people show up— 300 more than expected. They obviously didn't want to take no for an answer. We had a line around the block, and upset a few people who could not get in, even to the overflow rooms we had arranged. For almost every area of business, that day was a great learning experience.

SELL THE BIG PICTURE— DON'T THINK YOUR EMPLOYEES ARE MIND READERS

Businesses are nothing more than a group of people with a common goal and a feeling of purpose. With all the information and advice available on good management, businesses have no excuse for having counterproductive management practices. Yet most do. To create a great business, you must first have a vision and develop this common purpose.

This means that, as a business leader, you must:

$ Help your people to buy into the company's future

$ Show them how the culture of the company works and how you expect things to be done. Don't let them find out by trial and error, or make them guess

$ Get everyone to share in the excitement and the satisfaction and show them they'll be rewarded if the vision is fulfilled

$ Get a commitment from people—and make one yourself——to take and accept responsibility

$ Share the stress and the workload

$ Create a fun environment to help your people enjoy the struggles of the journey

$ Celebrate success and reward good work—even the small wins

$ Show that you respect your people, care about them, and appreciate what they do

Your employees all need nurturing. When you create an environment like this in your business, offering them respect and leadership, you bring out the best in them. Their feelings and reactions to working with you become "we love it here"—and when this happens, you get magical results.

Share the Vision

Winston Churchill's speeches are still remembered and still quoted today, especially the speech of the Battle of Britain: "We will fight them on the beaches . . . we shall never surrender . . ." Apart from being a great speech, it is remembered because it brilliantly communicated a vision of a country's purpose—to endure and prevail.

Sharing the vision is an important part of creating a great company culture. That means that you have to sell the big picture, your vision, at every opportunity.

It's essential to constantly share your vision, your goals, and your dreams with all your people.

It's essential to constantly share your vision, your goals, and your dreams with all your people.

You may be excited about your dreams, but you can't assume your people are. Remember, your business culture will depend on how strongly your people share your vision and excitement. This is how you get the best out of your people. They must feel they are part of creating something bigger than themselves; it gives them something and someone to believe in.

You must share with them where you are now and go to great lengths to explain how you intend to get where you are planning to go. Most importantly, you need to tell them how important *they* are in that process, the vital roles they will play, and what rewards and satisfaction they'll receive when you all get there together.

People need to know the vision and feel part of it. They need to know that their job, no matter how big or small, is integral to getting the whole team to the goal.

You have to communicate this in a realistic and genuine way that they understand. And it must be achievable—or the excitement you create will have a short shelf life. If your people discover you have sold them a load of hot air, then the game's over, you've lost, and you'll never get their commitment again.

After you have sold the vision, you must show them the steps you will take to get there, when all this will begin, and when it will finish. This isn't just a nice thing to do—it is essential, if you want a switched-on, motivated team of people who love their jobs and feel challenged and important. People like that will come to work happy to contribute, be creative, and stay until the job is done, not just until the clock strikes 5 P.M.

It's no good having a plan and assuming everybody knows what it is.

It's no good having a plan and assuming everybody knows what it is. It's not enough to go over your plan once in a while. Your job is to constantly sell your vision over and over again, with enough passion and conviction that employees cannot believe for one minute that it will fail. Do this and you won't fail, because if they believe in your vision they'll achieve it.

Are You a Great Leader, or Just the Boss?

Thousands of words have been written on leadership. Yet leadership is still a quality that few people seem to possess or even know how to practice.

Leadership is not a single skill, so it's difficult to study and define it. Leadership involves applying many of the ideas I have already covered: commitment, honesty, care, strong values, uniqueness, and much, much more. To be successful, however, you also need to lead people to where you want to go. But this can't be done without helping them get where *they* want to go at the same time.

Central to achieving this is respect of your people. You can't demand or buy respect; you must earn it by setting an example of all those things I've already mentioned. Things like ability, courage, loyalty, fairness, and honesty—and above all else, consistency. The example you set leads us to the golden rule of leadership: *Never ask anybody to do something you would not do yourself.*

Notice I said, "ask," not "tell." Your people will do only what you do, not what you say, so be careful of your actions, because they really shout (not speak) ten times louder than your words.

I've seen companies with quality signs and mission statements everywhere, but where the boss constantly pushes staff to cut corners and won't pay for any training. I've consulted to a firm where managers play computer games in front of their staff while

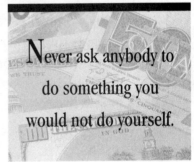

Never ask anybody to do something you would not do yourself.

it struggles to meet deadlines. On the other hand, I've also read about and seen magnificent examples of hands-on leadership. People like Nobel Peace Prize winner Albert Schweitzer, who backed up his humanitarianism by spending his life helping the sick in Africa. Or Bill Gates, a man with talent and a huge commitment to getting things done: a quality that runs through all of Microsoft.

CHAPTER 28

How to Hire the Right People

Employing people is easy—anyone can do it, but hiring the right people is another matter altogether. It's so important that it's up there with marketing as something for which you, as CEO, must be responsible.

Remember how I wrote that your people are your business? Why would you let anyone else be responsible for hiring when people are the basis of your success or failure? The first thing you can do to hire the right people is to do it yourself.

The first thing you can do to hire the right people is to do it yourself.

One thing that makes this process difficult is that the right person for one business may be totally inappropriate for another. This is the biggest problem in checking references to see if someone is any good. A particular person might thrive in one situation, and be great at what they do, yet be entirely unsuited to the next position.

It happens all the time. Many factors affect a person's performance and motivation, and for each person these factors are different. Some people thrive under pressure; others prefer a calm environment. Some like it fast, some slow, some loud, some quiet, some organized, some chaotic. Your chal-

If you hire someone great, you become great, and your life becomes easier.

lenge is to find the right person for your environment and culture. And every business is unique in this regard.

David Ogilvy, in his book *David Ogilvy on Advertising*, prudently advises people to use the Russian doll principle when hiring people:

When hiring people, Ogilvy suggests that you always hire bigger and better people than you, and you'll end up with a company of "giants." If you hire people smaller than you, you'll end up with a company of "dwarves." When he said this, he wasn't referring to their physical size, of course; he was referring to their skills, their integrity, and their ability.

This advice is right on the nose. If you hire someone great, you become great, and your life becomes easier. Hiring the wrong person will make your life and work harder and more frustrating, and it will make you look very bad. If you make the wrong choice—which is easily done—cut your losses as quickly as you can and start again.

BE A GREAT GARDENER— WEED QUICKLY AND REGULARLY

When you're hiring for a senior or important position, one that can affect the performance of the whole business, make sure you test people's skills and commitment before hiring them. For example, try scheduling interviews before or after hours and you'll quickly discover how serious, committed, and flexible the applicants are. This may sound crazy, but it's

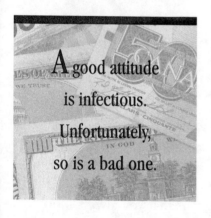

A good attitude is infectious. Unfortunately, so is a bad one.

surprising how much this sort of test will tell you about someone. Especially if they don't flinch at the news of the interview time and show up looking fresh and relaxed.

You can use this in your business, no matter how big or small, to test someone's attitude and ambition for work. It can be fun, and it will tell you more about them than firing a few tricky questions at them in a conventional interview.

As much as you'll try, however, there is no doubt that from time to time you'll make a mistake and hire the wrong person. If this is the case, don't wait any longer than you have to before replacing them. A good attitude is infectious. Unfortunately, so is a bad one. If you have failed with your attempts at adjusting his attitude, you must weed him out as soon as possible.

HIRE ONLY THOSE WITH A SPARKLE IN THEIR EYE

Although ideally you are looking for someone with particular skills, you are often well served by employing someone whose skills may be slightly less developed, and making his new job an exciting challenge. From that, he'll feel honored that you have given him trust and responsibility.

In most cases, if you have found someone with the right values and work ethic, he will not only raise himself to the challenge but will often go beyond it. And when he succeeds in doing a great job—which he will because he'll try harder, work longer, and be more dedicated and motivated—he will admire and respect you and become your most ardent supporter and loyal employee.

If you take these steps often enough—doing it yourself, hiring giants, testing applicants, and showing faith, you'll end up with a team of positive, enthusiastic people. And all of them will love their work, love the company, and happily drag you through the rough periods.

Get Good People, Then Hold On Like Hell!

I f you choose the right people, and you constantly challenge them and help them grow in skill and confidence,
you build your business in the best possible way.

You get people who enjoy their work, and you get loyalty in great measure. And if you treat people at every level
with respect, care, and kindness, you'll get that back, too.
All this contributes to the sort of workplace that does all the
things I've talked about in this book—all the things that
make your business work. That's why these people are your
greatest asset, and it's why you have to do everything you
can to keep them.

IT PAYS TO UNDERSTAND
AND REWARD

Every employee has emotions that she can't just check at the
door when she arrives for work. That even includes you.

Everyone in a business needs care, encouragement, reward, recognition, and, most of all, understanding.

Many businesspeople often use these words too commonly and too flippantly. The real value to your employees, and to your business, is delivered only when you provide these things genuinely. It may be difficult or uncomfortable for you, especially if you haven't consciously done this sort of thing before, but being sincere about caring for people and recognizing their successes is central to keeping a good staff.

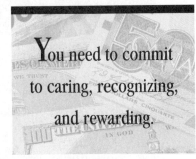

You need to commit to caring, recognizing, and rewarding. You need to make these habits part of you, your culture, and your values. When you love what you do and are excited about your work, it's easier to make that commitment. If you care, it's natural to focus on and recognize good work. It becomes natural to genuinely let the good performers know you appreciate them. And it doesn't have to cost a lot.

It can be done with a simple "thank you" or "well done." It can be as cheap as a memo or e-mail message. It can be a handwritten card, or best of all, it can take the form of public recognition at your next staff or sales meeting. A small gift or token of appreciation is sometimes a good idea, but isn't always necessary. What's more important is the genuine nature of what you're doing.

Whatever you do in applying these principles, be consistent and don't play favorites. Recognize, reward, and show appreciation for good results regardless of who achieves them, or all your efforts may be in vain.

Michael Leboeuf, in his book *The Greatest Management Principle in the World,* describes the key to achieving peak performance as rewarding only the action, outcome, or activity that you desire the most—and nothing else. Look again at how you are paying and rewarding people, because this could be your problem. Perhaps your reward system (financial or otherwise) is out of sync with the objectives you desire.

For example, examine the common idea of paying employees by the hour, without any incentive for performance. This practice actually rewards people for working slowly. Ask yourself why anyone would worry about the speed or efficiency of their work if they got the same reward for doing less. It makes no sense. But should you cling to this practice just because the alternatives may be difficult or socially unacceptable?

How to Make Yourself a Star

At Vision we developed a wonderful system of reward and recognition. It works well and gets everyone involved in the process of recognizing good work and good performance. The objective is a little different—to try to catch someone doing something "right."

When I thought about this idea, I thought implementing it would be difficult and impractical. When you have a lot of employees, and a lot going on, the challenge is to catch people doing things "right" when you are busy. If you're so busy yourself, how do you notice all of the great work being done out of your direct view? The answer is that you can't possibly be everywhere all the time. But others are! So we invented the Vision STAR Awards system.

Remember when you were at school, and did well, your teacher gave you a star? Well, as crazy as it might sound, we revived that seemingly infantile system. The only difference was that anyone at Vision could give anyone else a star—as a "thank you," as a reward for exceptional work, or as a recognition of work above and beyond the call of duty. This could be peers recognizing peers, managers recognizing subordinates, or a subordinate recognizing a manager. It was cross-departmental, too.

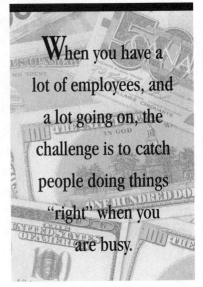

When you have a lot of employees, and a lot going on, the challenge is to catch people doing things "right" when you are busy.

It could be for any positive act: helping a team member, coming up with a creative idea, working long hours to meet a deadline, consistently producing high-quality work, providing exceptional customer service, saving the company money, or caring about someone else's emotions.

Team members nominate and award each other, even colleagues from other departments or their managers. Anybody catching someone else doing something right had the pleasant duty to speak up at weekly staff meetings and award a star.

The procedure involved the general manager making a mini-presentation of the star. The star was then publicly displayed at that person's desk or workstation. Material rewards were related to the stars that were accumulated. For example, five stars entitled you to a full-body massage, eight stars a dinner for two anywhere. Fifteen meant a weekend away for two in a five-star hotel. Staff could select another treat if they preferred.

The interesting thing is that we did this every week and gave out hundreds of stars over the years, yet only a few people collected the treats they earned. The reason is that for these people the stars and the public recognition were more important than the material reward. They loved getting them and displaying them for others to see, and this was the main motivation. They didn't really want to give them up in exchange for anything else.

CHAPTER

Always Use All of Your Resources, Including Your Entire Brain Pool

No business can afford to underutilize any of its resources. And if you have a staff of two, five, or fifty people, there is a huge resource at your disposal that may be underused—the imagination and experience of those people.

Many businesses put employees into a box determined by their job description, and then leave them there. This is nothing but a waste. People must fulfill their job descriptions, but they can offer so much more if you give them the opportunity.

Every business stems from an idea, and ideas come from people. Your next jackpot product, brilliant system, marketing inspiration, or production improvement will probably come from your people—not from consultants and probably not from you. Your employees are a tremendous resource of talent it pays to mine.

Every business stems from an idea, and ideas come from people.

A janitor of a huge twenty-four-hour automated robotics factory was encouraged to provide ideas to help the company save money. His idea, one might think, would relate to cleaning the factory. On the contrary, it was something far more simple than that, yet management had not seen it, even though it would save them tens of thousands of dollars a year. His idea: to turn off the lights that were burning twenty-four hours a day. Robots don't need light to work.

HOW TO UNLEASH AMAZING CREATIVITY

Walt Disney was one of the first people to reward creativity, not results. An employee tells of Mr. Disney introducing a bonus system offering $5 for a gag that was used in a picture, and $100 for an idea for a whole cartoon.

To get people to contribute their imaginative ideas to your business, the key is to give them ownership and responsibility, and then reward what contributions they make. The contributions don't even have to be successful just so long as you *never* penalize them for honest mistakes. Trust in their capacity to perform and support them if they have problems. If you've given someone a task beyond their skills, it's your job to help them develop those skills. All this gives them the latitude to grow and flourish, and to express their ideas— many of which will be practical and profitable.

This process cannot be the reckless release of creativity for its own sake. You have to have all your performance-measuring systems in place and monitoring what everyone's doing. This ensures your own efficiency and gives staff the feedback they crave on their performance. With trust, help, and clearly set goals, you'll be surprised what happens to your results.

TRAIN YOUR PEOPLE AS MUCH AS YOU TRAIN YOURSELF

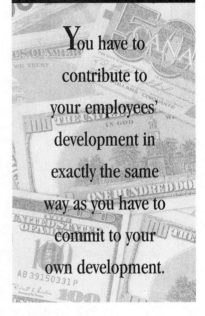

You have to contribute to your employees' development in exactly the same way as you have to commit to your own development.

Personal Foundations are essential for you as a business entrepreneur—they give you a starting point to develop yourself and your business to its fullest potential. It's exactly the same for your staff.

You have to contribute to your employees' development in exactly the same way as you have to commit to your own development. As the key resource in your business, the more they know, and the more they can do, the greater their contribution will be.

One of my clients runs an ad agency with a staff of twenty-five. He spends a fortune training copywriters and strategic planners to be the best they can. He sends them to interstate and overseas courses. He subscribes to every trade magazine that he can. He allocates training time each week. Not only does his staff produce great work, but its members also stay with him in the long term, which in advertising is quite rare.

It's bizarre that in tough times the training budget is one of the first things to be cut. It's in these times that improving

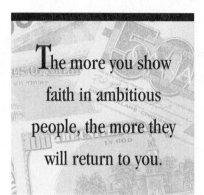

your people is even more important. Never make the mistake of seeing training as optional—it's one of the key advantages that your business has left, and it's what puts you ahead.

The more you show faith in ambitious people, the more they will return to you.

It's interesting to note that McDonald's lost money for the first seven years they traded in Australia. This occurred even with all the strength, resources, and knowledge of the U.S. parent company. What has made the Australian franchise now one of the most profitable is a reduction in menu choice and a large commitment to ongoing training.

It took time for the training to pay off, but it paid off in a big way.

LOOK OUT FOR A SHOOTING STAR

An ambitious employee is one who will give you more than you would ever expect. Even when you treat all employees with respect and care, some will still harbor more ambition and drive than others. When you see that and it's pretty clear, give the employee more opportunities to contribute and prove himself. The more you show faith in ambitious people, the more they will return to you. And even if their ambition takes them out of your business, they'll still love you for giving them their chance.

Wayne Pearce, the former Australian football player and now coach, talks about keying into people's ambitions. He doesn't walk into a dressing room before a game and start yelling to motivate people. His secret is that he gets to know each of his players well and understands what motivates each individual. Some will respond to shouting, others will respond to a quiet word at the right time. In order to indulge ambition in business, it's exactly the same. You also must tailor your motivation to the person and know him as a person before you get the best from him.

CHAPTER 31

If Two People Think the Same, One's Redundant

One thing that is always a change, when you move from being a technical expert to being a manager, is that you will need to deal with people who are different from you. Some people never even realize that this is the case. Believing everyone is the same, and treating them that way, shows a real lack of experience and leadership, and shows that you don't understand your employees.

You must realize that everyone is different, values different things, and is motivated in different ways. It's your job as the leader to work out what those ways are as soon as possible.

HIRE FOR THE JOB, NOT FOR YOUR EGO

It's human nature that people tend to like people who are similar to them or have similar likes to theirs. It's nothing to be ashamed of, because it is quite normal. It becomes a problem only when you start hiring employees because you like them, rather than because they are the best candidates for the job.

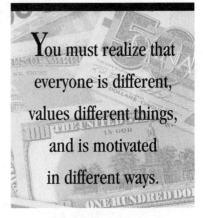

You must realize that everyone is different, values different things, and is motivated in different ways.

Early in my career I hired someone I liked. It went well for a while, and I enjoyed the conversations I shared with him, but ultimately it was a disaster. He wasn't suited for the job, and, because it was a job in market research dealing with data, I relied on him to give me accurate information—and he couldn't. What was worse was that I had to let him go, when it was really my fault for hiring the wrong person in the first place.

When hiring people for your business, the only similarities needed are in values, work ethic, and attitudes. You need to ensure that you share a common company culture, and you don't need similar personalities to do that.

SQUARE PEGS, ROUND HOLES

One of the most valuable lessons I've learned from rich people is to hire people I think are great as soon as I meet them, even if I don't have a clear job for them to do. I'll create a job for them because I want them on my team.

Now I know that some businesspeople can't always do that, but what *is* in your power is how you treat the workers you have. When you see a worker who isn't suited to a job—for example, a people person dealing with figures all day—

think of ways to change their job so that it does suit them. It's worth the effort. Once you have a great worker, you want to keep them as happy and productive as possible. You're cutting your own throat by forcing someone good to do something they don't love. You wouldn't do it, so why should they?

> It's worth the effort. Once you have a great worker, you want to keep them as happy and productive as possible.

The most common example of a mistake made in this area is promoting your best salesperson to become your sales manager. These are two completely different jobs, needing completely different skills, and a great salesperson usually is not a great manager. Do this and you lose out on both counts. You'll lose a great salesperson and the revenue they generate, and you'll have to sack your new sales manager—all through your own mistake.

PART **FIVE**

Your
Systems

CHAPTER 32

Why Systems Are
So Important

Systems are one of the four competitive advantages you have. They may be defined as a set of procedures or steps that you place into your business to ensure a predictable outcome each time. Drawing on your experience, learning from trial and error, or using meticulous planning, you can use systems to maximize your efficiency and minimize waste.

When you work on your business, as opposed to in it, you'll develop systems in all areas of your business: sales, marketing, production, distribution, and so on. Over a period of time, your business should become a well-oiled machine, needing only an occasional adjustment for changes in the market, the competitive environment, or your customer demand.

Systems offer you the unique opportunity to get the freedom you went into business to achieve. With systems thinking, you can make sure that you implement and maximize all the good business ideas you have, every time. Systems allow you to pass high-value work to others, allowing you to expand your focus and what your business does. And more than anything else, systems allow you to use *leverage* to gain success faster than you could imagine.

Making the Complex Seem Easy—and How to Sell Your Business Quickly, Easily, and at a Huge Profit

G reat customer service is vitally important if repeat customers are an integral part of your business—and I hope I've convinced you by now that they must be. The more reliant you are on repeat business, the better your customer service must be. In particular, businesses with necessary repeat business, such as restaurants, must have consistently great customer service or they'll have a very short life.

The only things that determine the quality of your service and the amount of your repeat business are:

$ The quality of your systems
$ The attitude of your people and the training they have received

Your systems are critical to making complex repetitive activities simple and easy. Systems and procedures, setting out what staff have to do, how it's done, when it's done, and so on, allow you to ensure consistent quality and performance. And you can do that every time, with complete predictability. With that consistent quality comes great service and more repeat business.

Good systems allow you to have complex tasks performed by less-skilled, less-experienced workers. They make your business less reliant on the individual and more reliant on the process of machinery and procedures. And it's unfortunate, but true, that procedures are much more reliable than individuals. A major benefit of this, and one that makes you money, is that it's easier to attract and train staff, because there are more lower-skilled workers than highly skilled ones.

Another of my clients provided printing and presentation materials. He was a great salesman for the industry and cared about his clients, but he couldn't let anyone else go out and meet them. He didn't trust other salespeople's knowledge or approach. At my urging, he drew up customer contact checklists and procedures and supported them with intensive training, including role plays. By giving salespeople a system to follow, he could begin to trust that they'd

> Your systems are critical to making complex repetitive activities simple and easy.

do a good job. Now the systems, training, and procedures have given him twelve salespeople (rather than one) and a business that is thriving without his ongoing involvement.

Making Money Out of Systems

Systems reduce the cost of running your business. You will have highly skilled results being produced by lower-cost labor, and you will have increased efficiency because people will know what to do, and they'll do it well. This is a kind of leverage in your business that is critical to building financial success.

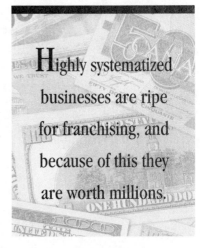

I'll discuss the concept of leverage next, but for the moment I should say there is no better way to leverage your business than to have good systems. They add value to your processes and produce a higher-value product at a much lower price. In other words, it is a very profitable practice.

Highly systematized businesses are ripe for franchising, and because of this they are worth millions. McDonald's is a classic example. By having procedures that are fixed and simple, they can employ the lowest-skilled labor they can find and know that the work will still be of good quality. And with that system, they can set up anywhere and know exactly what to do to succeed.

Essentially, systems allow your business to operate and function independently of you and become a business that produces profits without your own personal perspiration. This makes such a business a cash machine. And cash machines are very saleable assets that investors pay big bucks to get their hands on. That's why McDonald's is worth billions.

CHAPTER 34

Leverage: A Word That Makes People Millionaires

You now know the importance of systems and their impact on customer service, staff skills, and added value. I describe this effect as a kind of leverage.

It's important to realize that there are many other forms of leverage, and the word itself is used in many different ways. Financiers, for example, consider leverage to be the use of loan moneys to buy shares in a business or other assets that will give a greater return on the money borrowed than the rate of interest charged—thus making a profit. But leverage has a wider meaning when we use it to refer to less obvious assets in a business—such as time, marketing, and systems.

How do we use leverage in these areas to become rich? Everybody has the same twenty-four hours in a day, yet some people manage to earn an enormous amount and become very rich by using leverage well. They do this by leveraging themselves in every aspect of their lives. They make their time, their money, their marketing, and their systems all work for them, so they get more out of each. Leveraging is about duplicating a high-value item or skill at a much lower cost.

Time Leveraging

Let me give you a simple example of time leveraging. If you sell your time at, say, $20 per hour and you work twelve hours per day, the maximum you can earn is $240 per day—not bad money. But what if you were able to teach less skilled people to do what you do and pay them $10 an hour instead of $20? You can do this by providing them with easy systems and procedures you have developed.

Just having one person working your system, you are making $120 per day, which is less than before. But now you can spend your time—say, twelve hours a day—selling their time. For example, if you sold four of those people's time at $20 per hour (because they are producing $20 per hour worth of work) and still paid them only $10 per hour, you'd be making $480 profit per day (4 × $120). You have leveraged yourself from earning $20 per hour to $40 per hour, while working the same number of hours.

This is a basic point, but one that's critical if you want to be rich. Selling your own time will never make you rich. You must always develop systems and use someone else's time to produce something you can sell at a higher price.

Marketing Leverage

Here's a different example of leverage. If you are running an advertisement in a newspaper and, on average, that ad brings you ten sales at $1,000 per sale, that is $10,000 in total sales. If, however, you change the appeal of the advertisement with a great USP (see page 125) headline, and get eighteen sales per advertisement, you have leveraged this ad by $8,000. You are now receiving a much bigger reward for the same cost. This is an example of marketing leverage.

There are many others. For example, if your salespeople are converting one out of five leads into a sale, and through training and systems this increases to two out of five, you double your sales. And that comes with a small additional cost.

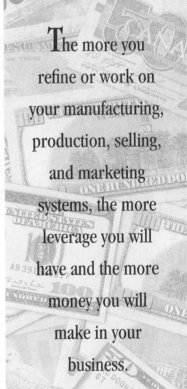

The more you refine or work on your manufacturing, production, selling, and marketing systems, the more leverage you will have and the more money you will make in your business.

If you send out direct mail, change your offer, and get a 30 percent better response, this is also a form of marketing leverage you can work on.

Systems Leverage

Systems are a great way of leveraging, too. As we know, systems are an essential way of making highly skilled or repetitive, high-cost processes easy and simple—allowing you to offer high-value products or services at a much lower cost. This is what a good business allows you to do.

What all this means is: The more you refine or work on your manufacturing, production, selling, and marketing systems, the more leverage you will have and the more money you will make in your business.

Take a look at the most successful people and businesses you can find. Dissect how they operate in each and every case. I guarantee that you will find they are highly leveraged in their finances, time, marketing, or production processes. Take McDonald's as an example again. What do you find? I don't know about their finances, but everything else they do is about getting the most out of the least effort, from leveraged production to leveraged marketing, which they're constantly testing and improving.

Focus on Money-Making Activities and Delegate to Others

A s you get to understand leverage in your business, it will become clearer that you should do the things only you can do. You must rely on your systems to help others do the rest. If a business isn't a success, often it's because owners and managers forget to focus on doing only the things that make the most difference and delegate the rest.

When you own or operate a business, especially a small business, you have many responsibilities and many chores. In this situation the golden rule is: *Never do anything you can pay someone else less money to do.* In business you should never spend your time doing anything other than the highly skilled work of developing and refining your systems or generating revenue through sales and marketing systems. Focusing solely on these two activities is what will make you the money you are seeking. Why? Because these are the two most highly leveraged things you can do with your time. By doing that you are making your business earn your income, rather than you selling your time. It's financial lunacy to do any work when you can get someone else to do it for less than you can earn elsewhere.

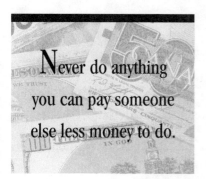

Never do anything you can pay someone else less money to do.

You might think you're saving money by doing some typing or going to the bank, but believe me, it's false economy and it's actually costing you much, much more because you are losing possible profits. It is foolish to think you can't afford it.

I know this may be difficult to do, especially when starting out in business or when finances are tight, but you must not get caught in the trap of trying to do it all yourself and thinking you are saving money.

HAVE FREEDOM AND STILL BE IN BUSINESS

Only time, money, and marketing leverage will give you the freedom you sought when you first started in business.

With leverage you can build your business and then step back and let it run itself. But in doing that, you won't be backing away from the business itself. You must keep an eye on systems, keep an eye on marketing, and keep an eye on all the business—but through the work you have done on your systems, you'll have the time to do what you want as well.

Problems Will Happen— But Only Once

O ne of the most important elements of your business systems is how you change them. We've seen how the world, the economy, and your customers are changing—your systems have to be able to adapt to match those changes.

As part of your systems you should build in a process for updating them. Continuous improvement or constant feedback ensures whenever a system doesn't perform adequately it's recorded, considered, and fixed.

It's the same when a problem appears for the first time. If your systems record what the problem was, and why it happened, you can create procedures or deliver training to make sure it doesn't happen again. That's the sort of thing that makes your service extraordinary.

COMPLAINTS ARE A GOLD MINE

I'm in a superannuation fund that sends me regular reports on my investment. After the first year of receiving reports

Customer complaints are the perfect method of gathering information.

I couldn't understand, I wrote them a letter explaining that I simply couldn't understand what they were saying. Two days later I got a letter thanking me for my contribution and letting me know they were already redesigning the statement. When I got the new statement a month later, it was great.

What happened here is that this insurance company listened to customer complaints and improved their business. Now I know I wasn't the only complainant, but the fact that they listened meant they had information they didn't have before.

Customer complaints are the perfect method of gathering information. It's cheap, you don't have to search for the information, and it immediately points out where you can do better. All you have to do is set up a system to record and act on those complaints. Tie it in with your continuous improvement system. Display the complaints to all your staff. Even inform your customers in a newsletter of what complaints you've received and how you fixed them. But never let a complaint go by without responding to it and benefiting from it.

CHAPTER 37

Measuring Performance: It's Not Nice, It's Critical

When I ask people relevant questions about their systems, measurement, and current performance of their business—not just the monthly profit and loss but their sales conversion ratios, their average transaction value, their inquiry rates, their lead generation rates, the performance of their advertisements, their return rate or cancellation rate, their lost sales rate, and so on—I usually hear, "We don't have that information." Most people don't know, or don't know how to measure, their performance, their staff's performance, or their business success factors. When a measuring system is put in place, they are usually amazed at the results. Usually they are performing far worse than they imagined.

If you don't know how your current resources, assets, and systems are performing, how do you know where to focus your attention and how to prioritize your resources? I've said that business is about people, but it's also about using information to reach people. If you don't have that information, you're not in the game.

You should know what your return on investment (ROI) is on everything that you do. I showed you the calculation of ROI on advertisements in a previous chapter (see page 158). This type of measuring must be done every time dollars are allocated to a resource. The same sort of measurement applies to staff performance. In the example, the measures of daily and weekly sales performance show who is making you money and who is costing you money. From this information you can give adequate feedback to your staff, make management changes, and, if you have to, change your staff.

COLLECT ONLY INFORMATION YOU NEED

Sometimes there can be a danger in measuring too many parts of the business. You can start to collect too much information, analyze too many things, and spend too much time and too many resources in the measuring process, and still not get the answers you need.

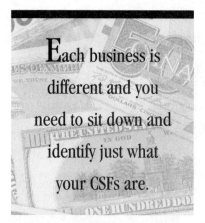

Each business is different and you need to sit down and identify just what your CSFs are.

The way to avoid this is to identify your business's Critical Success Factors (CSFs). These are the key things that determine your performance, your revenues, and your profits. You may have heard of them as Key Performance Indicators. Whatever the name, each business is different and you need to sit down and identify just what your CSFs are. And then measure only them and nothing else.

I saw one company manager produce 346 reports a month. He had two staff members devoted to producing these management reports. When I asked him how many his bosses looked at, he glanced at his desk and told me, "Four." The other 342 sat in folders until they were archived. The two staff members were soon doing better things with their time.

CHAPTER 38

Are You Gambling Your Profits Away?

If you had $1,000 and that's all you had, would you walk into a casino and risk it all on one roll of the dice? Chances are you wouldn't, especially if you didn't understand the rules of the game you were betting on. This, however, is exactly what people in business do every day. Whether you have done your research or not, everything you do you must *test first!* This draws on the same issues I talked about with measuring and developing information. You can't do things well if you don't know anything about them.

When I first learned about the importance of testing, it became an exciting and liberating experience. It's just so obvious that you should test all of your ideas in a small and controlled way and see what happens. If the idea works, adopt it and roll it out. If it doesn't, you haven't lost the farm. You can shut it down and try something else.

No one, not even the smartest or most experienced businessperson, can guarantee that any new project or idea will work. So testing is your key to protecting yourself and maximizing your returns. Test everything. Test new products, new systems, new marketing ideas, selling processes, customer service ideas, Magic Experiences, advertisements, and promotions—everything.

Do your research before you implement, but test when you implement. This allows you to take risks—and risk-taking is the way of winners. With testing you can take small risks and test to see if you have found a successful product or campaign—and if it is, back it heavily.

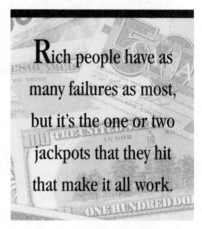

Rich people have as many failures as most, but it's the one or two jackpots that they hit that make it all work.

People looked at our successes at Vision Publishing and thought we took huge risks. But the truth is we tested everything and backed those that paid off. Each sales letter we used was tested in small samples. We ran the layouts of the summaries past a small group of customers before we changed anything. Each brochure layout and each headline was tested, the sales response was recorded, all of it was compared, and the best one was rolled out.

Systems become important in testing because testing can cause major unrest and disruption within an organization. Your systems need to be flexible, and you need to have a flexible, open-minded staff.

Testing Makes You Free to Fail

Failing is part of succeeding and should never be considered a personal fault. If you're not out there trying, testing, and accepting failure on the road to success, you're not trying hard enough. Rich people have as many failures as most, but it's the one or two jackpots that they hit that make it all work. Unfortunately, many businesses won't accept failure as a positive sign and sack people for failing when, often enough, those people should have been praised for trying.

What testing does is allow you to generate good ideas and feel free to try them out. If it's wrong, you find out quickly and little damage is done. This means you're still open to get your hands on that jackpot I was talking about.

Everyone Should Know Your Business

Former United States President John F. Kennedy was famous for being able to rally the nation with precise but stirring messages. Former President Ronald Reagan was known for his friendly, homespun stories that people could hang onto. President Bill Clinton is seen as someone who can tell people exactly what they need to hear. What all these presidents have in common is that they made communication the central part of what they did.

So far we've talked about systems as being ways of making the most of money, marketing, leverage, and information. And they're all incredibly important. But communication is the other area that has to be systematized to make your business work.

With good, reliable, and efficient communication in your business, you'll be able to share your vision with your employees without even trying. You'll be able to instill your values, recognize good performance, and do all the other things necessary to involve and motivate your employees. How you do it is up to you—meetings, newsletters, announcements, lunches, informal chats—but make sure it's part of a system. Systematic communication is what these presidents did—all in a different way—and it's what made them memorable as presidents, despite anything else that they may have done.

CHAPTER 40

Acres of Diamonds— Look Under Your Feet First

There was a wonderful book written by Russell Conwell in 1915 called *Acres of Diamonds*. It's certainly worth reading, now as then, because people in business today still make the same mistake he pointed out all those years ago, which is: They always tend to believe there are diamonds in someone else's backyard and should set up over there to seek their fortune rather than properly "prospecting" and "mining" their own patch.

Daily I come across people in business who find it tough. They often mistakenly think there must be something wrong with the customers or their market. They start to believe the next state or country is more fertile ground with bigger and better opportunities. Sadly, this is completely wrong.

Unless you wish to go and live in another state or country, it is business suicide to think you'll make it work better somewhere else, especially other than where you live. You should only expand your business to another region, state, or country after you have a strong home base to fund your growth. Doing business elsewhere is costly and distracting, and you simply cannot afford to do it without first achieving success in your home market.

PART SIX

Things to Remember

Growing Too Quickly Could Mean Getting Too Big for Your Boots

Although it's fun and exciting to grow, growing too fast can also kill you. It can be just as difficult, stressful, and frustrating to grow too quickly as it can be to grow too slowly. In my own businesses and those of my clients, I have experienced phenomenal growth rates of between 110 percent and 300 percent each year, and it has been extremely difficult in many cases.

Growing too quickly drains your time, energy, and resources—and you risk letting your standards slip, hiring the wrong sort of people, and creating a culture of "anything goes." Important details are overlooked, and mistakes that you ordinarily don't make start to happen.

You can quickly outgrow your systems and find you are so busy dealing with administration issues that you lose sight of where you're going. If you are breaking new ground every day, you can lose sight of your traditional market or long-established and loyal customers. You can alienate the

If you are breaking new ground every day, you can lose sight of your traditional market or long-established and loyal customers.

people who helped give you your start and were your best supporters when you needed them most.

You can also start to undermine your profits by overpaying because you need it now and you don't have the time and resources to shop around.

You end up hiring unsuitable people because you don't have the luxury of waiting to find the right person. But most importantly you are in danger of runaway overhead, which will leave you with a bigger operation but the same, or lower, level of profits.

Don't be seduced by "big is always better," and aim at strong, consistent growth. Anything else can eat into what you've already achieved.

CHAPTER

Trust Can Be a Four-Letter Word

Trust is a great attribute to have in life, but it has no place in business. You cannot rely on another person's goodwill for your success, no matter who they are and how trustworthy you think they may be. This also applies to doing business with family or friends.

That sounds horribly cynical, but if you follow it you can't go wrong. You have much to lose in trusting people in business—it's a minefield for the naive. You risk years of hard work going to waste, your security being undermined, and your reputation being ruined. It is simply not worth the risk.

It saddens me to say, but in business a completely trustworthy person is more often the exception than the rule. I speak not only from my experience, but also from the countless stories I have heard from those who have been too trustworthy in their business life.

If you think I'm going a little over the top and think this can't happen to you, simply go to a courthouse on any day and find out for yourself. People's perception of things changes when money is involved, especially substantial sums of money. So cover yourself with clear and well-prepared legal agreements, and document all important conversations and arrangements you have with people. With this approach there can be no misunderstanding later on, and you protect yourself and your future.

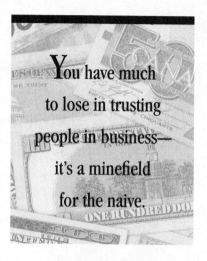

You have much to lose in trusting people in business— it's a minefield for the naive.

I know when going into an arrangement that you cannot conceive of being ripped off by the very person you are going to work with. It may be difficult to ask for guarantees; this displays a certain degree of mistrust on your part. But you are well advised to discuss these issues openly and up front, and if there is a lot at stake, get a lawyer involved. If the other party is indeed honest and trustworthy, they won't fear your insistence on this.

THE LAW CAN DO ONLY SO MUCH

You can't rely on the legal system to protect you—those who will take advantage of you also know how to beat it, or to at least play the legal system to their advantage. What you can do is minimize your risk by investing some time to find quality legal and accounting advice. It's important to review all aspects of your personal and business affairs, right through to proper workplace agreements with even your most trusted staff.

Make sure every agreement is clear and fully understood, and do not skimp on having a commercial lawyer advise you. Ensure especially that an exit strategy is clear, should things go wrong. This is never something anyone wants to discuss at the beginning of a relationship, but it is a big mistake not to have an agreement with an exit clause. This applies no matter how big or small your business may be or how much you trust the other person. The legal costs will save you in the long run.

AN ILLEGAL FAVOR ISN'T WORTH THE RISK

When you're in business, there are legitimate ways to maximize your income and minimize your tax. Never fall into the trap of thinking you are doing an employee a favor by slinging them a few extra dollars in cash. It may save you both a small amount of tax, but it exposes you to risks you needn't run. If your relationship sours, for example when you need to reprimand them for poor performance, they may forget about the "favor" you did them, and you may find yourself in court or in legal trouble with the government.

CHAPTER 43

You Don't Have
to Go It Alone

Business, especially small business, can be a lonely place. On many occasions people in business find they are stuck, or have run into some problem, or perhaps are entering territory they have not been in before.

Who can you turn to? You may find it difficult to turn to your spouse, staff, or friends because they may not have the

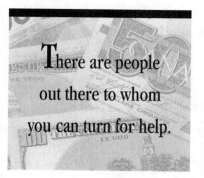

There are people out there to whom you can turn for help.

insight or experience to help you. This can be a very lonely time for a business owner or manager or anyone else attempting to start something new, be it a new project or a new job. This is when frustration and stress can get the better of you. Remember that even the most highly paid

executives in large companies have colleagues and directors they can turn to for help.

You don't have to go it alone. There are people out there to whom you can turn for help. If you're in this situation, it will most likely feel as if you have the world on your shoulders, carrying a heavy weight around. You cannot continue like this forever—it's detrimental to your business and your health. Take the step now to get some professional help. Even if it costs you some money, it's worth it.

You Cannot Create
Successful People

The most amazing paradox I have experienced is: Those who need help the most won't pay the price!

When I started Vision, I had about thirty active consulting clients. I made a list of those who were doing well and those I knew were still struggling. I sent each of them a subscription application to the Vision Business Book Summaries. I guessed they were seeking business help in one form or another and that summaries would be a great tool for all of them to learn from. I put a cross next to each person I thought would subscribe.

As the return mail arrived over the next few weeks, I was astounded. I couldn't have been more wrong. I had predicted that the strugglers would subscribe. It was amazing to see that exactly the opposite had occurred. It was those who were in fact doing well who had subscribed—and not a single struggler.

What does this say about those who were doing well? There is probably a reason behind their success—the same reason that is behind the failure of the others. People who ultimately succeed in life are those who recognize early on that success is a state of mind and has nothing to do with their current level of financial assets. Success comes in direct proportion to a person's ability to recognize this, and his or her willingness to pay the price.

I learned then that you cannot create successful people, you can only take successful people and help them become more successful. Success is not always externally obvious—it may be just a feeling inside someone or a spark in their eye.

Everything you have read in this book so far will not work for you unless you already have what it takes. You may not have the external signs of success or wealth yet, but this book and the ideas it contains will help you get there a lot more quickly. Anyone without the spark wouldn't have bought this book in the first place, and that says a lot about you.

> **P**eople who ultimately succeed in life are those who recognize early on that success is a state of mind and has nothing to do with their current level of financial assets.

To combine your special drive and ambition with what you've learned about the importance of *you, your marketing, your people,* and *your systems* is the most you can do to ensure success.

Adaptation from Desiderata

Go placidly amid the noise and haste and remember what
peace there may be in silence.

As far as possible be on good terms with all people. Speak
the truth quietly and clearly and listen carefully to
others, even the dull and ignorant, they too have a
life story.

Avoid loud and aggressive persons, they are vexations to
the spirit. Never compare yourself to others, you may
become either vain or bitter, for there will always be
greater and lesser persons to you.

Enjoy your achievements as well as your plans. Keep
interested in your own career, however humble, it's
a real possession in the changing fortunes of time.

Exercise caution in your business affairs, as the world is
full of trickery.

Be true to yourself, do not feign affection. Neither be
cynical or blinded by love, for in the face of aridity
and disenchantment it is as perennial as the grass.

Find somebody to love, love what you do, and always
be excited about your future. When you find love
give nothing but love, yet demand none in return.

Be a true friend, as being a friend is a gift you give to yourself.

Take kindly to the passing of the years, gracefully surrendering the things of youth, but never your health.

Nurture your strength of spirit to shield you from misfortune, but do not distress yourself with imaginings. Many fears are born unnecessarily out of fatigue and loneliness.

Spend your time wisely, and only in the company of those that matter, as time is the only true currency you have.

Beyond a wholesome discipline, be kind and gentle with yourself. Remember you are a child of the universe, no less than the trees and the stars. You have a right and a special purpose in being here. Whether it is clear to you or not, the universe is unfolding as it should.

Therefore be at peace with yourself and your god, whatever you conceive it to be. Whatever your labors and aspirations, keep peace with your souls in the noisy confusion of life.

With all it's shame, drudgery, and broken dreams, it is still a beautiful world.

Be cheerful, be happy.

Bibliography

Collins, James C. & Porras, Jerry, I. *Built to Last: Successful Habits of Visionary Companies.* HarperBusiness, 1997.

Conwell, Russell H. *Acres of Diamonds,* Jove Publications, 1995.

Covey, Stephen R. *The 7 Habits of Highly Effective People: Powerful Lessons in Personal Change.* Fireside, 1990.

Dyer, Dr. Wayne. *You'll Believe it When You See It.* Avon, 1990.

Gerber, Michael. *The E Myth Revisited: Why Most Small Businesses Don't Work and What to Do About It.* HarperBusiness, 1995.

Getty, J Paul. *How to Be Rich.* Jove Publications, 1996.

Hill, Napoleon. *Think and Grow Rich.* Ballantine Books, 1996.

Kennedy, Dan S. *How to Succeed in Business by Breaking All the Rules: a Plan for Entrepreneurs.* E P Dutton, 1997.

Le Bouf, Michael. *The Greatest Management Principle.* Out of print.

Maltz, Dr. Maxwell. *Psycho-Cybernetics.* Pocket Books, 1987.

Ogilvy, David. *Oligvy on Advertising.* Random House, 1987.

Index

About the Author

Brian Sher was born in South Africa and moved to Australia in high school. He obtained a degree in marketing from the University of New South Wales, and developed and launched a successful baby-care product.

His subsequent business travels overseas sparked his interest in consultancy, and after spending two years in Los Angeles he returned to Australia and formed his own company specializing in marketing and business-growth strategies. Working with businesses both big and small, one of his major clients offered to partner with Brian in a new venture—Vision Publishing.

Under Brian's direction, Vision Publishing experienced phenomenal growth, and ultimately boasted over $12 million in annual sales. Brian's extensive network and strong reputation as one of Australia's most dynamic and exciting marketers make him an active and sought-after business coach. He divides his time between Sydney and Los Angeles.